Vocabulary Mastery Book B

Third Edition

Gene Stanford
John A. Rothermich
Barbara Dodds Stanford

Phoenix Learning Resources, LLC

Phoenix Learning Resources, LLC

914 Church Street • Honesdale, PA 18431
1-800-228-9345 • Fax: 570-253-3227 • www.phoenixlr.com

Item# 2193   ISBN 978-0-7915-2193-9

Table of Contents

Table of Contents *continued*

PREFACE

Let's be realistic about vocabulary study. Learning words cannot guarantee you admission to college or propel you toward automatic success. But knowing the meanings of important words can be useful. If a word you don't understand keeps cropping up in your reading, you must stop to look it up or sacrifice understanding the text. If you find yourself having to make do with a general word like *nice* or *pleasant* because you don't know a more specific word, you may feel frustrated, and your speaking and writing will lack precision.

Vocabulary study, therefore, can be of value to you if the words you learn are commonly used in the kind of reading you'll be doing or will help you say what you mean in more interesting ways. Learning the meanings of obscure words may make you feel sophisticated but will do little to enhance your ability to read and communicate.

VOCABULARY B is a book that avoids the pitfalls of teaching obscure words. It presents words that have use in the real world. It requires that you learn only two words per lesson and furnishes you with what you need to know about using the words.

After reading the explanatory matter, you confront two kinds of practice with the new words. In the first kind of practice (Exercise A), you test your ability to *recognize* the meanings of the words as you must do when you encounter them in reading a magazine or a newspaper article. In the second kind of practice (Exercise B), you test your ability to *recall* the words and use them in the proper way. This practice prepares you to use the new words in your own speaking and writing.

Words from previous lessons keep showing up in the practice exercises, and so you never have a chance to forget them. By devoting ten minutes a day to this kind of vocabulary study, you will take command of approximately two hundred useful new words as well as hundreds of synonyms and antonyms of the vocabulary words.

But that's not all. As a bonus, this book includes lessons that introduce you to more than forty Latin and Greek word parts on which several hundred English words are based. Learning these word parts will give you the keys to the meanings of countless other unfamiliar words.

lesson 1

spite ■ picket

spite	(n)	(spīt)
ORIGIN:	Latin *despectus* (a looking down upon)	
MEANING:	Petty ill will with the desire to irritate, annoy, or thwart another	
CONTEXT:	"Billy showed *spite* toward his cousin by calling him ugly names."	
SYNONYMS:	malice, ill will, spleen, grudge	
ANTONYMS:	benevolence, kindness, goodwill	
OTHER FORMS:	spite (v), spiteful (adj.), spitefully (adv.)	

picket	(v)	('pik-ət)
ORIGIN:	Middle French *piquet* (a stake)	
MEANING:	To place protesters around a factory, store, or building, as during a strike or demonstration against policies, practices, or actions	
CONTEXT:	"Many *picketed* the Russian Embassy because they did not like Russia's policy toward Iran."	
SYNONYMS:	demonstrate against, protest against	
OTHER FORMS:	picket (n. or adj.)	

A. Focus on Meaning

Circle the letter of the best meaning for each vocabulary word.

1. spiteful: a) happy   b) restrictive   c) malicious   d) hopeless

2. picket: a) demonstrate against   b) compete   c) retire   d) remove

3. spite: a) observe   b) annoy   c) study   d) accept

4. spite: a) happiness   b) shyness   c) ability   d) ill will

5. picket: a) protester   b) corridor   c) courtyard   d) family

6. picket: a) display   b) encourage   c) praise   d) march against

B. Words in Context

Supply the proper form of the most appropriate vocabulary word.

picket   spite

1. The freshmen stomped their feet when the principal entered the auditorium to _____ her for insisting that they sit together in the front section.

2. The freshmen class officers said they would _____ the principal's office if she continued to insist that they occupy those seats.

3. To react with _____ toward a school requirement is foolish behavior.

4. The _____ might be suspended from school.

5. Would you be willing to join a(n) _____ line in front of the office?

6. I would have to feel _____ to do so.

Shades of Meaning

- spite
- ill will
- rancor
- malice
- grudge

lesson 2

agile ▪ swagger

agile   (adj)   (ˈaj-əl)

ORIGIN:	Latin *agilis* (easily moved)
MEANING:	Able to move quickly and easily
CONTEXT:	"Maria is a very *agile* girl and should be an excellent athlete."
SYNONYMS:	nimble, lithe, athletic, graceful
ANTONYMS:	awkward, clumsy, sluggish
OTHER FORMS:	agility (n.), agilely (adv.)

swagger   (v)   (ˈswag-ər)

ORIGIN:	Norwegian dialect *svagga* (to sway)
MEANING:	To walk or strut with a defiant or arrogant manner
CONTEXT:	"The conceited young man *swaggered* into the room and propped his feet up on the coffee table."
SYNONYMS:	strut, parade
OTHER FORM:	swagger (n.)

A. Focus on Meaning

Circle the letter of the best meaning for each vocabulary word.

1. agile: a) easily upset   b) nimble   c) generous   d) brave

2. swagger: a) strut   b) bow one's head   c) praise   d) predict

3. spiteful: a) thankful   b) young   c) curious   d) mean

4. agility: a) freedom   b) length   c) litheness   d) promptness

5. picket: a) demonstrate against   b) ask questions of
     c) give reasons for   d) ignore

B. Words in Context

Supply the proper form of the most appropriate vocabulary word.

agile   picket   spite   swagger

1. A group of employees, carrying posters calling for better wages and working conditions, will _____ the store beginning on Tuesday.

2. The _____ of antelopes helps them to escape from their enemies.

3. After losing the race to Sylvia, Sammie acted _____ toward her.

4. Sylvia's _____ and her boastful attitude did nothing to help restore her friendship with Sammie.

5. My grandmother, who often defeats younger women at tennis, is quite _____ at seventy.

6. The new student _____ into the dressing room and began boasting about what a good basketball player he was.

7. Have you ever watched a squirrel move from tree to tree through the upper branches? Their _____ is truly amazing.

defect ▪ mortify

defect   (n)   (ˈdē-ˌfekt)

ORIGIN: Latin *deficere* (to fall short)

MEANING: A fault or an imperfection; a lack of something
               essential for perfection

CONTEXT: "The sweater has been reduced in price because of
               a *defect* in the sleeve."

SYNONYMS: blemish, flaw, imperfection

ANTONYMS: perfection, supreme excellence, flawlessness

OTHER FORMS: defective (adj.), defectiveness (n.), defectively (adv.)

mortify   (v)   (ˈmȯrt-ə-ˌfī)

ORIGIN: Latin *mortificare* (to put to death)

MEANING: To humiliate, to shame

CONTEXT: "Mary was *mortified* when her sister caught her
               peeking through the keyhole."

SYNONYMS: humble, abase, shame, humiliate

OTHER FORMS: mortification (n.), mortifyingly (adv.)

A. Focus on Meaning

Match each word with its synonym by writing the proper letter in the blank.

1. defect _____

2. mortification _____

3. agile _____

4. defective _____

5. mortify _____

6. swagger _____

a) nimble   b) strut   c) having a flaw   d) humiliation   e) blemish   f) shame

B. Words in Context

Supply the proper form of the most appropriate vocabulary word.

agile   defect   mortify   spite   swagger

1. Jeff's _____ over spilling paint on his new shirt was so great that he asked the principal for permission to go home and change clothes.

2. Young deer are usually clumsy leapers; they develop _____ only through much practice.

3. Articles selling at lower prices as "irregulars" are _____ in some way.

4. The _____ of the umpire as he returned to home plate suggested that he thought he was very important.

5. It would surely _____ my aunt if she thought you knew she dyes her hair.

6. Having a(n) _____ in hearing, Cynthia Smith asked for a seat near the front of the room.

7. The Murphy twins get along so well that I have never heard them say one _____ word to one another.

8. Alice's table lamp does not turn on; she thinks this is caused by _____ wiring.

lesson 4

grim ▪ sovereign

grim (adj) (grim)	**sovereign** (n) (ˊsäv-[ə]-rən)
ORIGIN: Old English *grimm* (fierce)	ORIGIN: Old French-Middle French *soverain* (a king)
MEANING: Harsh and forbidding in appearance or character, ghastly	MEANING: A ruler or a person who has supreme authority or rank, being above all others in power or importance
CONTEXT: "Both the dark brick house and the old man living in it present such *grim* appearances that the children are careful never to trespass on the property."	CONTEXT: "Shah Mohammed Reza Pahlavi was the *sovereign* of Iran."
SYNONYMS: harsh, unyielding, hideous, horrible, severe, dreadful	SYNONYMS: monarch, potentate, emperor
ANTONYMS: attractive, gentle, inviting	OTHER FORM: sovereignty (n.)
OTHER FORMS: grimly (adv.), grimness (n.)	

A. Focus on Meaning

Circle the letter of the best meaning for each vocabulary word.

1. sovereign: a) storage place b) monarch c) peasant d) throne room

2. grim: a) dreadful b) hopeful c) pleasant d) weak

3. sovereignty: a) need for change b) decent wages c) supreme power d) sturdiness

4. defect: a) slope b) blemish c) trash container d) explosion

5. grimness: a) minor improvement b) hideousness c) shame d) reluctance

B. Words in Context

Supply the proper form of the most appropriate vocabulary word.

agile   defect   grim   mortify   sovereign   swagger

1. Death is often spoken of as the _____ reaper.

2. Morocco has a(n) _____ who is both the king and the highest officer in the government.

3. Because porcupines are not _____ and cannot flee from enemies, they are equipped with quills and spines to protect themselves.

4. The situation of the castaways as they floated for days on their small life raft looked pretty _____.

5. Have you noticed the way in which Elise and Manuel _____ into class since their election to the student council?

6. Sheila was _____ when she mistakenly loaned Helen the _____ sleeping bag for the camping trip.

7. State troopers too often have the _____ task of responding to highway traffic accidents.

lesson 5

afflict ▪ valor

afflict	(v)	(ə-ˈflikt)		**valor**	(n)	(ˈval-ər)

afflict (v) (ə-ˈflikt)

ORIGIN: Latin *affligere* (to cast down)

MEANING: To trouble or to distress so greatly as to cause continued suffering

CONTEXT: "Mother is so *afflicted* with arthritis in her hands that sewing is very painful for her."

SYNONYMS: vex, harass, torment, plague, distress

ANTONYMS: comfort, console, aid

OTHER FORMS: affliction (n.), afflictive (adj.)

valor (n) (ˈval-ər)

ORIGIN: Latin *valere* (to be strong)

MEANING: Determination and boldness in facing danger

CONTEXT: "My father received a medal for *valor* in the Korean conflict.

SYNONYMS: courage, bravery, heroism

ANTONYMS: cowardice, faintheartedness, fearfulness

OTHER FORMS: valiant (adj.)

A. Focus on Meaning

Circle the letter of the best meaning for each vocabulary word.

1. afflict: a) torment   b) cure   c) give away   d) explain

2. valor: a) shyness   b) bravery   c) roughness   d) leadership ability

3. grim: a) powerful   b) courageous   c) cowardly   d) horrible

4. affliction: a) translation   b) discussion   c) anger   d) distress

5. valiant: a) necessary   b) dreadful   c) courageous   d) impressive

B. Words in Context

Supply the proper form of the most appropriate vocabulary word.

> agile   afflict   defect   mortify   valor

1. Job, an Old Testament character, was _____ with boils over his body.

2. The _____ in the zipper led Lucy to return the jacket.

3. A story in today's newspaper describes the _____ of a local firefighter who entered a burning building to rescue the trapped tenants.

4. Ringworm, a contagious skin disease, is a common _____.

5. I won't forget the _____ I suffered at the hands of Elspeth Mudd, a self-styled comedian, who made me the butt of all her jokes and barbs.

6. The mayor made a speech praising the _____ of the scouts who saved a baby from drowning in Clearwater Lake.

7. Ginger Rogers and Fred Astaire moved effortlessly across the dance floor; no one had ever seen a dance team with such _____.

8. Prince _____ is one of the oldest running comic strips in the United States.

lesson 6

tumult ▪ gaunt

tumult	(n)	('t[y]ü-,məlt)		**gaunt**	(adj)	(gȯnt)

tumult (n) ('t[y]ü-,məlt)

ORIGIN: Latin *tumultus* (an uproar)

MEANING: Violent and disorderly disturbance with confusion

CONTEXT: "The *tumult* created by the crowd prevented the mayor from speaking."

SYNONYMS: disorder, commotion, agitation, uproar

ANTONYMS: order, peace, quietude

OTHER FORMS: tumultuous (adj.), tumultuously (adv.)

gaunt (adj) (gȯnt)

ORIGIN: English dialect *gant* (tall and thin)

MEANING: Extremely thin, haggard, and drawn as from great hunger, weariness, or torture

CONTEXT: "The *gaunt* man stumbled into the camp and feebly told how he had been wandering on the mountains for days."

SYNONYMS: spare, lank, raw-boned, scrawny, lean

ANTONYMS: stout, well-fed, sturdy

OTHER FORMS: gauntly (adv.), gauntness (n.)

A. Focus on Meaning

Match each word with its synonym by writing the proper letter in the blank.

1. tumult _____
2. gaunt _____
3. afflict _____
4. tumultuous _____
5. valor _____
6. gauntness _____

a) distress   b) disorderly   c) courage   d) thin   e) commotion   f) lankness

B. Words in Context

Supply the proper form of the most appropriate vocabulary word.

gaunt   grim   sovereign   tumult

1. Several people had been injured, but their cries for help were lost in the _____ of screeching air-raid sirens.

2. It is a(n) _____ fact that many people in the United States, the leading food producer in the world, are suffering from malnutrition.

3. The faces of the released prisoners of war were _____ and pale from torture and insufficient food.

4. Queen Bess was the _____ of the country, although a council helped her to govern.

5. Myra created a(n) _____ when she took her pet skunk to the picnic.

6. Maxwell, our Scottish terrier, returned home tired and _____ after being lost for several weeks.

Shades of Meaning
- gaunt
- spare
- lank
- raw-boned
- scrawny
- lean

Gaunt suggests marked thinness as from overwork or suffering. *Spare* suggests leanness from eating and drinking very little or constant exercise. *Lank* implies tallness as well as leanness. *Raw-boned* implies a large ungainly build without implying undernourishment. *Scrawny* implies extreme leanness and suggests lack of strength and vigor. *Lean* stresses lack of fat and curving body contours.

lesson 7

tassel ▪ negotiate

tassel (n) ('tas-əl)

ORIGIN: Old French-Middle French *tassel* (small buckle, a small, ornamental piece of fabric)

MEANING: A hanging ornament made of a bunch of cords of even length fastened at one end

CONTEXT: "The beautiful white horses in the parade wore blankets embroidered in gold and trimmed with silk *tassels*."

negotiate (v) (ni-'gō-shē-ˌāt)

ORIGIN: Latin *negotiari* (to do business)

MEANING: To arrange, confer, or deal with others in order to arrive at a settlement of some matter

CONTEXT: "Representatives from the two firms met for several days and finally *negotiated* a merger."

SYNONYMS: bargain arrange, deal with

OTHER FORMS: negotiable (adj.), negotiation (n.), negotiator (n.)

A. Focus on Meaning

Circle the letter of the best meaning for each vocabulary word.

1. grim: a) lacking color b) quiet c) dreadful d) cheerful

2. negotiate: a) bargain b) prevent c) inspire d) pretend

3. tassel: a) argument b) hanging ornament c) medieval dwelling d) large wave

4. tumult: a) uproar b) laughter c) bargain d) decision

5. negotiable: a) unfortunate b) unpleasant c) eternal d) open to bargaining

6. gaunt: a) spooky b) out of breath c) very thin d) wise

B. Words in Context

Supply the proper form of the most appropriate vocabulary word.

afflict	gaunt	grim	negotiate	sovereign	tassel

1. Originally a(n) _____ was a clasp with a bunch of cords hanging from a knob or head.

2. After years of fighting, both sides finally agreed to begin talks in an attempt to _____ a cease-fire.

3. Abraham Lincoln was a tall, raw-boned man with a(n) _____ face that gave him the appearance of a weary and half-starved refugee.

4. The high school seniors were told that they could buy the _____ from their caps when they turned in their caps and gowns.

5. AIDS is a _____ disease that sprang up in the twentieth century and now _____ millions of people around the world.

6. These days all professional athletes have agents who _____ their contracts with the owners.

7. Queen Victoria was the _____ of a British Empire that circled the Earth.

lesson 8

merge ▪ suspension

merge	(v) (mərj)	**suspension**	(n) (sə-ʹspen-chən)

ORIGIN:	Latin *mergere* (to plunge)	ORIGIN:	Latin *suspendere* (to hang up, to check)
MEANING:	To combine or unite	MEANING:	Temporary withholding as of belief, opinion, decision, privileges
CONTEXT:	"The two drugstores in our little village *merged* into one business in order to provide customers with a wider variety of products."	CONTEXT:	"After several months of fighting, both sides agreed to a *suspension* of hostilities during the Christmas season."
SYNONYMS:	unite, blend, consolidate	SYNONYMS:	postponement, deferment, interruption
ANTONYMS:	part, separate, divide	OTHER FORM:	suspend (v.)
OTHER FORM:	merger (n.)		

A. Focus on Meaning

Circle the letter of the best meaning for each vocabulary word.

1. merge: a) produce b) combine c) bow under pressure d) surprise

2. suspension: a) misty fog b) postponement c) chemical solution d) cable

3. afflict: a) harass b) expose c) reconsider d) beg

4. merger: a) cabinet b) highway c) uniting d) extraordinary experience

5. suspend: a) separate b) weave in and out c) defer d) offer support to

B. Words in Context

Supply the proper form of the most appropriate vocabulary word.

gaunt merge negotiate suspension tassel valor

1. The _____ of negotiations between the dog-catchers' union and the city was caused by the interference of the kennel club.

2. When Amy and I wanted to use the car at the same time, Dad had to _____ a settlement.

3. The _____ faces of the children of that coal-mining town show the effects of malnutrition.

4. The new drapes have black _____ to match the zebra-striped chair near the window.

5. The principal will probably _____ classes because of the blizzard.

6. Highways 24 and 31 _____ at the town limits to form Main Street.

7. The firefighters fought _____ to save the house in the path of the forest fire.

8. When Rick and Patti married, they worked hard to _____ each of their families into one.

lesson 9

Let's try an experiment. Do you know the meaning of *gregarious*? Chances are that you do not. You've probably never come across this word in your reading. Read the following sentence, and see what happens:

Bob's *gregarious* nature is evident in his love of parties, his friendly greetings in the halls at school, and his reluctance to spend a single evening alone.

Now do you know what gregarious means? Is Bob more likely to be considered: (a) a lone wolf   (b) social-minded   (c) a social outcast   (d) a show-off?

From this example, it is apparent that you can use the clues contained in the rest of the sentence—or the surrounding sentences—to determine the meaning of an unfamiliar word. In this case you were able to put together the qualities revealed in the three facts about Bob and guess that they all indicated a social-minded nature. Sometimes the clues are not so obvious as those in the example. Sometimes there aren't any clues. But frequently—if you are a good "word detective"—you can make a good guess at the meaning of a word based on the information contained in the surrounding words. Most clues fall into three categories:

1. Direct Definition: If authors of books realize that readers may not understand new or unusual terms, they often write definitions of new words into the text. For example:

   Few Americans are aware of how seriously pollution threatens to upset our *ecology*, the relationship between living things and their environment.

   Sometimes a definition is introduced by a phrase such as *that is* or follows a form of *to be*: Dr. Ehrlich pointed out that pollution has brought about serious changes in the *ecology* of the Earth. *Ecology* is the study of the relationship between living things and their environment.

2. Explanation and Examples: By "putting the pieces together"—as you did in the sentence about Bob—you get a general idea about the meaning of a new word. Often you will have to rely on your previous experience. Look carefully at this sentence:

   One thing that irritates students is *arbitrary* punishment, severe punishment given to one student and a light penalty given to another student who did the same thing.

3. Contrast: Sometimes a sentence reveals the meaning of a strange word by showing you its opposite. The construction of a sentence or some word or phrase such as *although, however, but, while,* or *on the other hand* indicates that the unfamiliar word is opposite in meaning to a word or phrase that you understand. For example:

   Although she was a little devil during the day, my little sister looked like a *cherub* when she was asleep.

Exercise: Examine the clues in the following sentences in order to understand the meanings of the italicized words. Then circle the letter of the best guess of the meaning for the italicized word.

1. *Incipient* tuberculosis is more easily cured than that which has progressed to an advanced state.

   a) curable   b) beginning   c) deadly   d) hard to detect

2. Janice's *duplicity* soon caused a problem. While assuring her mother that she was studying at a friend's home, she was going out with Dave, the boy her parents had forbidden her to see.

   a) persuasion   b) power   c) trickery   d) opinion

3. By threatening to tell her parents that she was seeing Dave, Pete was able to *coerce* Janice into lending him her favorite CD.

   a) force   b) beg   c) coax   d) lure

4. Except for a sense of satisfaction in serving others, Anna gets no *remuneration* for playing the organ for synagogue services.

   a) instruction   b) payment   c) opportunity   d) encouragement

5. Anna's instrument has twenty-seven *ranks*—that is, rows of pipes—each of which has its characteristic tone.

   a) positions of power   b) keys   c) skills of leadership   d) rows of organ pipes

6. Many students heap *adulation* on Joe because of his great athletic ability, but I find little else in him to admire.

   a) bunches of flowers   b) wealth   c) insults   d) praise

7. My grandfather has such a *phobia* about dogs that he will not take a walk unless someone goes along to prevent one from approaching him.

   a) allergy   b) loving attitude   c) fear   d) attraction

8. Jack *cowered* behind the couch, fearful of what his mother would say when she saw the broken vase.

   a) hid playfully   b) crouched fearfully   c) cleaned carefully   d) jumped energetically

9. Excessive eating has made Beth so *corpulent* that none of her clothes fits her any more.

   a) nervous   b) jolly   c) guilty   d) fat

Using Context Clues in This Book: In addition to giving you a way of guessing the meanings of unfamiliar words, a knowledge of context clues can help you work the exercises in this book. In the sentences in Exercise B, from which vocabulary words have been omitted, you should be alert to the clues that indicate what word is to be supplied. It is important that you read the sentences carefully, keeping in mind the various kinds of clues that can help you determine which word to place in the blank.

lesson 10

version ▪ cringe

version	(n)	(ˈvər-zhən)

ORIGIN: Latin *vertere* (to turn)

MEANING: A particular form, account, or variation of something

CONTEXT: "Mary's *version* of what happened in the room was quite different from Sue's."

SYNONYMS: impression, story, account

cringe	(v)	(ˈkrinj)

ORIGIN: Old English *cringan* (to yield)

MEANING: To shrink, stoop, or crouch, especially in fear

CONTEXT: "The dog *cringed* when the burly man approached, as though he suspected that the man would mistreat him."

SYNONYMS: flinch, cower, wince

A. Focus on Meaning

Circle the letter of the word in each group that does not belong.

1. a) variation   b) depression   c) version   d) form
2. a) cringe   b) flinch   c) cover   d) shrink
3. a) unite   b) separate   c) merge   d) consolidate
4. a) tassel   b) hoop   c) decoration   d) ornamentation
5. a) version   b) verse   c) story   d) account

B. Words in Context

Supply the proper form of the most appropriate vocabulary word.

cringe	mortify	negotiate	picket	suspension	version

1. The boy _____ when his father suggested a ride on the roller coaster.
2. To _____ a settlement generally requires that both sides give a little.
3. The coach reminded Elsa that her _____ from the team was a result of breaking training rules.
4. The King James _____ of the Psalms is more poetic than many modern translations.
5. Several real estate firms in our city have been _____ by civil rights groups because they discriminate against members of minority groups.
6. It is easy to understand Karen's _____ over failing geometry; up to now she has been a straight A student.

C. Antonyms

Circle the letter of the word whose meaning is most nearly opposite the vocabulary word.

1. merge   a) consolidate   b) unite   c) divide   d) bargain
2. defect   a) blemish   b) flawless   c) grudge   d) plague
3. spite   a) ill will   b) strut   c) sparkle   d) kindness
4. agile   a) athletic   b) lithe   c) comfort   d) awkward
5. afflict   a) torment   b) trouble   c) aid   d) promote
6. tumult   a) peace   b) uproar   c) disorder   d) blend

lesson 11

melancholy ▪ pollute

melancholy (adj) (ˈmel-ən-ˌkäl-ē)		**pollute** (v) (pə-ˈlüt)	
ORIGIN:	Late Latin *melancholia* (long-lasting mood)	ORIGIN:	Latin *polluere* (to soil, defile)
MEANING:	In a gloomy state of mind; depressed	MEANING:	To make impure, unclean, dirty
CONTEXT:	"Ramon became *melancholy* after the doctor told him he would have to remain in bed another week."	CONTEXT:	"Many of our rivers are *polluted* because waste materials have been emptied into them."
SYNONYMS:	dejected, sad, depressed	SYNONYMS:	contaminate, taint, befoul
ANTONYMS:	happy, cheerful, lighthearted	OTHER FORMS:	pollution (n.), pollutant (n.)
OTHER FORM:	melancholy (n.)		

A. Focus on Meaning

Circle the letter of the best meaning for each vocabulary word.

1. melancholy: a) sad   b) shaped like a melon   c) ignorant   d) painful

2. pollute: a) discourage   b) make dirty   c) fill with water   d) prevent

3. version: a) deer meat   b) dislike   c) clear eyesight   d) account

4. cringe: a) decorate   b) flinch   c) change   d) expire

5. suspend: a) postpone   b) put in motion   c) present   d) support

B. Words in Context

Supply the proper form of the most appropriate vocabulary word.

cringe	melancholy	pollute	suspension	tumultuous	valor

1. Although Nancy _____ at the thought of eating fried grasshoppers, her brother stoutly maintained that he was hungry enough to eat virtually anything.

2. Would a new puppy help to cheer Andy and lessen his _____ over the death of his old dog?

3. Many people argue that rock lyrics glorifying the use of drugs may _____ the minds of young people.

4. Many medals for _____ are awarded after heroes have died.

5. Fumes from cars, buses, and factories _____ the air in our cities.

6. The _____ old man, reflecting sadly upon happier days gone by, sat in a rocking chair on the porch of the nursing home.

7. The wind-driven waves at the shore were the most _____ that Courtney had ever seen in all her years as a lifeguard.

8. After the thunderstorm the golf match was _____ until Saturday.

lesson 12

somber ▪ indulge

somber (adj) (ˈsäm-bər)

ORIGIN: Late Latin *subumbrare* (to overshadow)

MEANING: Dark and gloomy; sad and grave

CONTEXT: "Monday was a dull, gloomy day, and Ruth was in a *somber* mood that matched the weather."

SYNONYMS: melancholy, depressing, dismal, dull

ANTONYMS: bright, cheerful

OTHER FORMS: somberness (n.), somberly (adv.)

indulge (v) (in-ˈdəlj)

ORIGIN: Latin *indulgere* (to be overly kind to)

MEANING: To yield to one's own desires or to the wishes and whims of another

CONTEXT: "Although she barely earned enough to support her family, Mrs. Simpson frequently *indulged* her taste for fine dining."

SYNONYMS: pamper, gratify, favor, humor

ANTONYMS: discipline, control, restrain

OTHER FORMS: indulgingly (adv.), indulgence (n.), indulgent (adj.)

A. Focus on Meaning

Match each word with its synonym by writing the proper letter in the blank.

1. somber _____
2. indulge _____
3. melancholy _____
4. somberness _____
5. pollution _____
6. indulgence _____

a) dismal   b) depression   c) gloominess   d) contamination   e) gratification   f) pamper

B. Words in Context

Supply the proper form of the most appropriate vocabulary word.

indulgent	melancholy	pollute	somber	swagger	version

1. The _____ appearance of the rundown clinic depressed the patients.

2. The driver's _____ of how the accident occurred was colored by his fear that his license would be suspended.

3. _____ grandparents often allow children to eat too many sweets between meals.

4. The furnishings used in horror films seem heavy and _____, creating a dismal atmosphere.

5. When the weather is cold and somber, I prevent _____ feelings by lighting a fire in the fireplace and playing lively music on the stereo.

6. Although detergents are cleaning agents, they are a major cause of _____ when they are pumped into waterways by careless manufacturers.

7. From his size it was easy to see that Frank often _____ his appetite for fast food.

8. The opposing center _____ onto the basketball court as if he owned the place.

9. The extended period of dark days and heavy rain has everyone in a _____ mood.

lesson 13

martyr ▪ imperative

martyr	(n)	(ˈmärt-ər)
ORIGIN:	Greek *martus* (witness to one's faith)	
MEANING:	One who sacrifices his life or something of great value for the sake of principle or devotion to a cause	
CONTEXT:	"Martin Luther King, Jr. was a *martyr* to the cause of social justice."	
SYNONYMS:	sufferer, victim	
OTHER FORMS:	martyrdom (n.), martyr (v.)	

imperative	(adj)	(im-ˈper-ət-iv)
ORIGIN:	Latin *imperare* (to command)	
MEANING:	In the nature of a command; not to be avoided or evaded	
CONTEXT:	"I realized that it was *imperative* to remain at home and help Mother because she was not feeling well."	
SYNONYMS:	necessary, essential, compelling, urgent	
ANTONYMS:	unnecessary, nonessential	
OTHER FORM:	imperatively (adv.)	

A. Focus on Meaning

Circle the letter of the best meaning for each vocabulary word.

1. martyr: a) sufferer   b) heavy cannon
                  c) cement-like filling between bricks   d) religious person

2. imperative: a) fruit-filled   b) essential   c) retarding   d) unable to function

3. somber: a) very old   b) highly seasoned   c) gloomy   d) exclusive

4. indulge: a) refuse   b) pamper   c) penetrate   d) bribe

5. martyrdom: a) brick building   b) indifference   c) death for a cause   d) observation

6. imperative: a) slow   b) doubtful   c) unrelenting   d) necessary

B. Words in Context

Supply the proper form of the most appropriate vocabulary word.

cringe	indulge	imperative	martyr	pollute	valor	version

1. Sarah's _____ in rich food at the picnic resulted in an upset stomach.

2. Thousands have died for their beliefs throughout history, but only a few have been honored for their _____.

3. The harmful effects of water _____ can be seen in Lake Erie where thousands of fish have died.

4. It is _____ that you submit a report to the principal on the meeting because your expenses were paid by the school.

5. The captain urged the crew, "Do not _____ from fear but set forth boldly with _____ in your heart."

6. Today it is absolutely _____ for students to know how to use a PC and how to use the Internet.

7. The _____ of Joan of Arc has inspired many book, plays, and movies.

8. There are still many questions about the _____ of Shakespeare's plays that we know today.

lesson 14

magnitude ▪ hurtle

magnitude	(n)	(ˈmag-nə-ˌt[y]üd)

ORIGIN: Latin *magnus* (great)

MEANING: Greatness in size, extent, influence, effect, or importance

CONTEXT: "The *magnitude* of the damage from the flood can hardly be imagined by someone who was not at the scene."

SYNONYMS: hugeness, immensity, greatness

ANTONYMS: smallness, minuteness, littleness

hurtle	(v)	(ˈhərt-əl)

ORIGIN: Old French *hurter* (to thrust)

MEANING: To move with great speed; to throw or fling

CONTEXT: "After breaking through the guardrail, the car *hurtled* down the mountainside."

SYNONYMS: rush, hurl, fling

A. Focus on Meaning

Circle the letter of the best meaning for each vocabulary word.

1. magnitude: a) minuteness   b) hugeness   c) magnificence   d) multitude

2. hurtle: a) hurdle   b) rush   c) injure   d) impress

3. martyr: a) sufferer   b) sponsor   c) sympathizer   d) agitator

4. magnitude: a) source   b) great size   c) circumference   d) latitude

5. imperative: a) essential   b) happy   c) useless   d) commanding

B. Words in Context

Supply the proper form of the most appropriate vocabulary word.

hurtle   indulge   magnitude   melancholy   somber

1. The boxcar _____ over the embankment and into the ravine.

2. Mother's new dress is less _____ than the ones she has been wearing since Father's death.

3. The _____ of the damage caused by the hurricane staggers the imagination.

4. If people _____ in cigarette smoking, they are more apt to get lung cancer.

5. Bricks, machinery, furniture, and debris were _____ through the air by the explosion in the factory.

6. The blast was of such incredible _____ that it broke windows and shook buildings as far as six miles away.

7. After the basketball team lost by two points in the state finals, the feeling around the high school was quiet _____ for several days.

8. It is almost impossible to grasp the _____ of the Milky Way Galaxy, much less the universe.

liberal ▪ humility

liberal	(adj)	(ˈlib-[ə]-rəl)
ORIGIN:	Latin *liber* (free)	
MEANING:	Open-minded; favoring progress and reform	
CONTEXT:	"That teacher has a *liberal* attitude toward new methods in teaching and is always willing to experiment."	
SYNONYMS:	progressive, advanced, broad-minded, tolerant, generous	
ANTONYMS:	intolerant, orthodox, hidebound	
OTHER FORMS:	liberalism (n.), liberality (n.), liberate (v.), liberation (n.)	

humility	(n)	(hyü-ˈmil-ət-ē)
ORIGIN:	Latin *humilis* (humble)	
MEANING:	The quality or state of being modest or unassuming	
CONTEXT:	"Dwight Eisenhower showed *humility* even though he was a famous general and a popular president."	
SYNONYMS:	meekness, modesty	
ANTONYMS:	vanity, arrogance	
OTHER FORMS:	humble (v. or adj.), humiliate (v.), humiliation (n.)	

A. Focus on Meaning

Circle the letter of the best meaning for each vocabulary word.

1. liberal: a) slanderous   b) open-minded   c) silly   d) stern

2. humility: a) haughtiness   b) fertilizer   c) solidness   d) humbleness

3. magnitude: a) unity   b) hugeness   c) florescence   d) opinion

4. liberate: a) free   b) constrain   c) identify   d) mock

5. humiliate: a) mortify   b) test   c) harness   d) indulge

B. Words in Context

Supply the proper form of the most appropriate vocabulary word.

humility   liberal   martyr

1. Ruth's _____ over having been late for dinner caused her to apologize profusely to Mrs. Jackson and the other guests.

2. More _____ in governmental policies may develop when some of the old leaders retire.

3. Joan of Arc was a fearless _____ who was burned at the stake because she acted on her religious convictions.

4. That our city councilors have become more _____ in their attitudes is evidenced by the fact that they now issue permits to hold rock concerts in the park.

5. _____, not arrogance, is a characteristic of great leaders.

Shades of Meaning

- liberal
- progressive
- advanced
- broad-minded
- generous

lesson 16

layman ▪ repulse

layman   (n)   (ˈlā-mən)

ORIGIN: Greek *laihos* (of the people)

MEANING: One who is not a member of the clergy or a member of a specified profession

CONTEXT: "Many churches reserve certain Sundays when *laymen* lead the services and pastors sit with their congregations."

SYNONYMS: parishioner; amateur

ANTONYMS: clergy; specialist

OTHER FORM: laity (n., plural)

repulse   (v)   (ri-ˈpəls)

ORIGIN: Latin *repellere* (to drive back)

MEANING: To drive back; to drive away by discourtesy or rejection

CONTEXT: "John *repulsed* every attempt that I made to be friendly by ignoring me."

SYNONYMS: repel, reject, rebuff

OTHER FORMS: repulsion (n.), repulsive (adj.)

A. Focus on Meaning

Circle the letter of the best meaning for each vocabulary word.

1. layman: a) one who lays bricks   b) one who preaches   c) one who builds churches   d) one who is a member of a congregation

2. repulse: a) accept   b) repair   c) reject   d) release

3. liberalism: a) rejection   b) intolerance   c) modesty   d) broad-mindedness

4. repulsion: a) acceptance   b) attraction   c) rejection   d) remittance

5. laity: a) the clergy   b) lawyers   c) builders   d) parishioners

B. Words in Context

Supply the proper form of the most appropriate vocabulary word.

hurtle   layman   magnitude   repulse

1. The waiter's rudeness and arrogance were so _____ to the tourists that they left without ordering breakfast.

2. Some doctors believe that _____ do not understand medical terms, and, therefore, they do not try to explain their methods of treatment.

3. The _____ of the damage done to citrus crops will be felt by consumers who will have to pay higher prices for fruit.

4. Although numerous attacks on the Alamo by the Mexican army were _____, the fort finally fell on March 6, 1836.

5. Suddenly, one of the racing cars _____ off the track and burst into flames.

C. Antonyms

Circle the letter of the word whose meaning is most nearly opposite the vocabulary word.

1. gaunt   a) scrawny   b) stout   c) clumsy   d) gentle

2. liberal   a) generous   b) progressive   c) orthodox   d) fearless

3. melancholy   a) lighthearted   b) dejected   c) sad   d) restrained

4. indulge   a) restrain   b) return   c) pamper   d) humor

5. somber   a) depressing   b) dull   c) attractive   d) bright

6. imperative   a) important   b) necessary   c) urgent   d) nonessential

lesson 17

For many years you've known that a number of longer English words result from putting together two or more shorter words. A *fingerprint* is the "print" that a "finger" makes; a *scarecrow* is constructed to "scare" away "crows". Knowing the meanings of the basic elements (the short words) gives you the keys to understanding the compound words that they make up.

Similarly, if you know the meanings of the basic word elements that we have borrowed from Latin and Greek, you can take apart longer words built on these elements and interpret their meanings. Your interpretation will not always be precise, but when you combine it with other clues found in the sentence, you will be guided toward making a correct guess of the meaning of an unfamiliar word.

Basic elements or word parts are of three kinds:

1. those placed at the beginning of a word (prefix)

2. those forming the main part of a word (root)

3. those placed at the end of a word (suffix).

As an example, look at the word *unsuccessful*. Notice that it can be divided into three parts:

1. un- (a prefix meaning "not")

2. success (a familiar word)

3. -ful (a suffix meaning "full of")

By knowing the meanings of these three parts, you understand the long, unfamiliar word: "not full of success."

Here are the two word parts for this lesson. You are given the origin of each part, the meaning or meanings, and a sample word in which this part appears. If the word part can be spelled several ways, these versions are listed under Other Forms.

-less (suffix)	
ORIGIN:	Old English *leas* (free, loose)
MEANING:	Without, lacking
CONTEXT:	"hope*less*"

un- (prefix)	
ORIGIN:	Latin *in* (not)
MEANING 1:	Not
CONTEXT 1:	"*un*happy"
MEANING 2:	Reversal of verb action
CONTEXT 2:	"*un*fold"
NOTE:	Do not confuse un- with the Latin word uni, which means "one," as in united.

lesson 17 continued

A. In each of the italicized words below, underline the word part that you have learned. Then, using your knowledge of the meaning of the word part, circle the letter of the best meaning for the italicized word.

1. the *dauntless* young woman:
   a) without fear   b) stingy
   c) jaunty   d) strong

2. *unsophisticated* girl:
   a) snobbish   b) not worldly wise
   c) intelligent   d) lonely

3. *matchless* skill:
   a) without equal   b) forgotten
   c) average   d) below average

4. *unwarranted* criticism:
   a) deserved   b) allowable
   c) not justified   d) desirable

5. *peerless* manners:
   a) without an equal   b) bad
   c) not necessary   d) showy

6. a *hopeless* situation:
   a) good   b) not desirable
   c) without hope   d) full of hope

7. *untangle* the yarn:
   a) put tangles into   b) wash
   c) discard because of tangles   d) take tangles out of

8. *undress* the child:
   a) bathe   b) remove shoes
   c) put on clothes   d) take off clothes

9. *helpless* animals:
   a) wild   b) tame   c) not needing help
   d) without the ability to care for themselves

10. an *unconfirmed* report:
   a) proved   b) not proved
   c) reported by one person   d) reported by many

B. Review. Match the correct definition to each vocabulary word. Write the letter of the definition on the line.

_____ 1. mortify   a. contaminate

_____ 2. agile   b. nimble

_____ 3. martyr   c. victim

_____ 4. negotiate   d. strut

_____ 5. spite   e. monarch

_____ 6. sovereign   f. humiliate

_____ 7. pollute   g. ill will

_____ 8. swagger   h. bargain

lesson 18

hoard ▪ horde

hoard	(v)	(hō[ə]rd)	**horde**	(n)	(hō[ə]rd)
ORIGIN:	Old English *hydan* (to hide)		ORIGIN:	Mongolian *orda* (a camp)	
MEANING:	To hide away for future use		MEANING:	A great multitude	
CONTEXT:	"Fearing that there would be a shortage, many people began to *hoard* sugar at the beginning of World War II."		CONTEXT:	"During the Democratic convention *hordes* of delegates poured into New York, occupying every available hotel room near Madison Square Garden."	
SYNONYMS:	accumulate, collect, amass, hide		SYNONYMS:	throng, crowd, mass, multitude	
OTHER FORMS:	hoarder (n.), hoard (n.)				

A. Focus on Meaning

Match each word with its synonym by writing the proper letter in the blank.

1. hoard (v.) ＿＿＿＿   2. horde ＿＿＿＿   3. layman ＿＿＿＿

4. hoard (n.) ＿＿＿＿   5. repulsive ＿＿＿＿   6. humility ＿＿＿＿

a) accumulate   b) nonspecialist   c) meekness   d) supply   e) repellent   f) crowd

B. Words in Context

Supply the proper form of the most appropriate vocabulary word.

hoard	horde	humility	layman	liberal	repulse

1. A(n) ＿＿＿＿＿＿＿＿＿＿＿ knows little about the finer points of the law and so depends on a lawyer when he or she needs advice or help on legal matters.

2. Have you ever watched squirrels ＿＿＿＿＿＿＿＿＿＿＿ nuts for winter by burying them in the ground?

3. The boys hoped that the girls would be ＿＿＿＿＿＿＿＿＿＿＿ by the dead rat outside the door and would not enter their clubhouse.

4. The Roman Empire finally collapsed when ＿＿＿＿＿＿＿＿＿＿＿ of barbarians poured out of the north and destroyed the remaining Roman legions.

5. Although Lucy's grandmother is quite a(n) ＿＿＿＿＿＿＿＿＿＿＿ -minded person about most things, she is very intolerant of short skirts on her granddaughter.

6. The actors who won Oscars showed great ＿＿＿＿＿＿＿＿＿＿＿, taking little credit for their accomplishments.

7. The novel, *Silas Marner*, tells about a lonely miser who ＿＿＿＿＿＿＿＿＿＿＿ his money and delighted in counting it every night.

8. Wherever Tiger Woods plays golf, he is followed by ＿＿＿＿＿＿＿＿＿＿＿ of fans.

lesson 19

lateral ▪ hereditary

lateral (adj) (ˈlat-ər-əl)

ORIGIN: Latin *latus* (side)

MEANING: Directed toward, coming from, or situated on the side

CONTEXT: "I had a *lateral* view of the building as I looked out the car window."

SYNONYMS: sidelong, sidewise

OTHER FORM: laterally (adv.)

hereditary (adj) (hə-ˈred-ə-ˌter-ē)

ORIGIN: Latin *hereditas* (heirship)

MEANING: Received from or transmitted from parent to offspring

CONTEXT: "That *hereditary* trait, blue eyes, is from the Hearn side of our family."

SYNONYMS: transmissible, ancestral, inheritable

OTHER FORMS: inherit (v.), inherited (adj.), heredity (n.), inheritance (n.)

A. Focus on Meaning

Circle the letter of the word in each group that does not belong.

1. a) lateral   b) sidelong   c) sidewise   d) center

2. a) hereditary   b) ancestral   c) heretical   d) transmissible

3. a) amend   b) amass   c) hoard   d) accumulate

4. a) lateral   b) one-sided   c) bottomless   d) sidelong

5. a) horde   b) throng   c) crowd   d) supply

6. a) heredity   b) inheritance   c) ancestry   d) herald

B. Words in Context

Supply the proper form of the most appropriate vocabulary word.

hereditary	imperative	laity	lateral	repulse	somber

1. Juan caught the _____ pass but was quickly forced out of bounds near the opponents' bench.

2. The _____, equally divided over the issue of whether to carpet the church, tried to get the minister to state a position on the matter.

3. When asked why he was always late to school, Jimmy replied, "Lateness must be a(n) _____ trait in my family; my parents never get to work on time."

4. My small dog has often _____ larger dogs by its fierce growling and barking.

5. Hemophilia, a(n) _____ disease, is transmitted from mothers to their sons.

6. The old house, dirty, dark, and overgrown with shrubs and trees, caste a _____ mood on the neighborhood.

7. The running back's sharp _____ moves left the defenders grabbing air.

8. If I want to get good grades it is _____ that I spend at least one hour studying every night.

lesson 20
knack ▪ haughty

knack	(n)	(nak)
ORIGIN:	Middle English *knak* (sharp blow)	
MEANING:	A talent or aptitude for doing something	
CONTEXT:	"Ann Landers has a *knack* for giving good advice about handling personal problems."	
SYNONYMS:	gift, ability, skill, dexterity	

haughty	(adj)	(´hȯt-ē)
ORIGIN:	Old French *haut* (high)	
MEANING:	Overly proud, snobbish	
CONTEXT:	"After she started attending that private school, Alice became a very *haughty* girl, often passing old friends without so much as nodding to them."	
SYNONYMS:	overbearing, lordly, disdainful	
ANTONYMS:	meek, modest, unassuming	
OTHER FORMS:	haughtily (adv.), haughtiness (n.)	

A. Focus on Meaning

Circle the letter of the best meaning for each vocabulary word.

1. knack: a) skill   b) pounding noise   c) importance   d) groove

2. haughty: a) cheap   b) having much weight   c) intelligent   d) proud

3. lateral: a) successful   b) reasonable   c) appropriate   d) sideways

4. knack: a) cap   b) hammer   c) ability   d) meekness

5. somber: a) bright   b) melancholy   c) made of straw   d) in a deep sleep

6. haughtiness: a) snobbishness   b) desperation   c) hatred   d) shyness

B. Words in Context

Supply the proper form of the most appropriate vocabulary word.

haughty	horde	hurtle	knack	magnitude

1. When I cleaned off Mother's desk and found the important papers that she thought had been lost, she said I seemed to have a(n) _____ for detective work.

2. My classmates were not favorably impressed by the new boy's _____ manner and swaggering walk.

3. When I opened my desk drawer, I was startled to see a(n) _____ of ants swarming over the candy I had hidden there.

4. Rebecca had a(n) _____ for flattery and could always get people to do what she wanted.

5. The _____ of the Grand Canyon never fails to amaze visitors.

6. The supermodel _____ stormed out of the store when the clerk did not recognize her.

7. The new Amtrack passenger train, the Ocelot, between Washington D. C. and New York City, _____ down the track at more than 120 miles per hour.

LESSONS 1–20

For each numbered word choose the word or phrase that is closest to the meaning of the vocabulary word. Write the letter for the word on the line provided.

1. agile   a) clumsy   b) aggressive   1. _____

     c) nimble   d) quick

2. valor   a) fearfulness   b) courage   2. _____

     c) distress   d) cowardice

3. indulge   a) pamper   b) restrain   3. _____

     c) discipline   d) strut

4. hoard   a) crowd in   b) abuse   4. _____

     c) harass   d) hide away for future use

5. spite   a) kindness   b) goodwill   5. _____

     c) parade   d) ill will

6. merge   a) separate   b) muddle   6. _____

     c) unite   d) divide

7. hereditary   a) overbearing   b) received from parent   7. _____

     c) ancestors   d) defective

8. grim   a) attractive   b) dull   8. _____

     c) harsh and forbidding   d) scrawny

9. pollute   a) depress   b) contaminate   9. _____

     c) reject   d) torment

10. cringe   a) flinch   b) distress   10. _____

     c) crank   d) soften

11. defect   a) flawless   b) perfection   11. _____

     c) flaw   d) destruction

12. tumult   a) quietude   b) peace   12. _____

     c) violent disturbance   d) strong temptation

13. imperative   a) unnecessary   b) dreadful   13. _____

                 c) athletic   d) essential

14. haughty   a) modest   b) overbearing   14. _____

                 c) unassuming   d) gentle

15. negotiate   a) torment   b) control   15. _____

                 c) project   d) bargain

16. magnitude   a) minuteness   b) magnificence   16. _____

                 c) hugeness   d) smallness

17. humility   a) modesty   b) vanity   17. _____

                 b) generosity   c) arrogance

18. repulse   a) release   b) repel   18. _____

                 c) arrange   d) shame

19. somber   a) cheerful   b) bright   19. _____

                 c) distress   d) depressing

20. afflict   a) torment   b) comfort   20. _____

                 c) aid   d) agitate

TEST TIPS

Sometimes vocabulary tests ask you to choose a synonym for the word being tested. A synonym, as you know from the lessons you have studied so far in this book, is a word with the same or nearly the same meaning. When you take such a test, study all of the choices and first eliminate answers that are clearly wrong.

Practice: In each sentence choose the synonym for the italicized word. Write your answer on the line.

1. In January the weather on Mt. Washington is nearly always *grim*.   1. _____

    (a) snowy   (b) sunny   (c) harsh   (d) changeable

2. The faces of the refugees were *gaunt* and anxious.   2. _____

    (a) fearsome   (b) strange   (c) troubled   (d) scrawny

3. The children grew *melancholy* when Prince, their new puppy, had to stay overnight at the animal hospital.   3. _____

    (a) restless   (b) depressed   (c) hopeful   (d) relieved

4. June has the *knack* of making at least 75% of her free throws in every basketball game.   4. _____

    (a) ability   (b) desire   (c) patience   (d) poise

lesson 21

smirk ▪ picturesque

smirk	(v)	(smərk)
ORIGIN:	Old English *smerian* (to laugh)	
MEANING:	To smile in an affected or offensive way	
CONTEXT:	"The rude passenger *smirked* at the bus driver who asked him to lower his radio."	
SYNONYMS:	simper, leer, snicker	
OTHER FORMS:	smirkingly (adv.), smirk (n.)	

picturesque	(adj)	(ˌpik-chə-ˈresk)
ORIGIN:	Latin *pictor* (painter)	
MEANING:	Resembling a picture, especially having wild beauty	
CONTEXT:	"Every summer my grandparents visit Sausalito, a *picturesque* little fishing village across the bay from San Francisco."	
SYNONYMS:	graphic , vivid, quaint	
ANTONYMS:	ugly, plain, drab	

A. Focus on Meaning

Circle the letter of the best meaning for each vocabulary word.

1. smirk: a) strike on the side of the face   b) leer   c) afflict   d) endanger

2. picturesque: a) artistic   b) tiny   c) of French origin   d) covered with paint

3. knack: a) ability   b) dissent   c) an African beetle   d) marshy area

4. smirk: a) scuffle   b) offensive smile   c) rebellious attitude   d) complete collapse

5. hoard: a) save   b) invent   c) spend   d) gamble

6. haughty: a) tall   b) shortsighted   c) snobbish   d) humble

B. Words in Context

Supply the proper form of the most appropriate vocabulary word.

haughty	hereditary	picturesque	smirk

1. Eureka Springs, Arkansas, is a small town of _____ charm that looks like a Swiss village.

2. The doctor's _____ manner made it seem as if she were doing me a favor by treating me.

3. The tourists stopped to admire and photograph the _____ dancers in native costumes performing in front of the sixteenth-century castle.

4. The _____ on our opponents' faces seemed to suggest, "There's no way you can win this debate."

5. Weak lungs can be _____, but tuberculosis cannot.

Shades of Meaning

- picturesque
- graphic
- vivid
- quaint

Picturesque suggests a striking or effective picture, often without regard to reality. *Graphic* stresses the evoking of a clear, lifelike picture. *Vivid* suggests a sharp impression of something vigorously alive. *Quaint* implies an old-fashioned but pleasant oddness about the scene.

lesson 22

-fer- ■ -port-

-fer- (root)

ORIGIN: Latin *ferre* (to bear or carry)

MEANING: To carry, bear, or yield

CONTEXT: "re*fer*"

-port- (root)

ORIGIN: Latin *portare* (to carry)

MEANING: To bear or carry

CONTEXT: "trans*port*"

A. Focus on Meaning

In each of the italicized words below, underline the word part that you have learned. Then, using your knowledge of the meaning of the word part, circle the letter of the best meaning for the italicized word.

1. *deportation* of an alien: a) carrying away   b) curiosity   c) arrival   d) arrest

2. *transfer* the cargo: a) place in a ship   b) remove from a ship
c) carry to another place   d) sell at a high price

3. *guiltless* of the theft: a) involved in the crime   b) carrying information
c) without guilt   d) having knowledge

4. a *portable* television set: a) manufactured near a seaport   b) a floor model
c) cannot be repaired easily   d) can be carried from place to place

5. *defer* a decision: a) make hastily   b) carry forward to another time
c) make without necessary information   d) ask for

6. an *unfeeling* person: a) sympathetic   b) free of pain
c) not caring   d) thoughtful

7. *transport* the troops: a) vaccinate   b) arm   c) carry   d) warn

B. REVIEW

Match the correct definition to each vocabulary word. Write the letter of the definition on the line.

_____ 1. picket   a. hide away

_____ 2. hoard   b. amateur

_____ 3. knack   c. ability

_____ 4. tumult   d. throng

_____ 5. lateral   e. sidelong

_____ 6. haughty   f. uproar

_____ 7. horde   g. overbearing

_____ 8. layman   h. demonstrate against

lesson 23

sheaf ▪ punctual

sheaf   (n)   (shēf)

ORIGIN: Old English *sceaf* (wisp of straw)

MEANING: Any bundle, collection, or cluster resembling or suggesting a bundle of grain

CONTEXT: "Put a rubber band around that *sheaf* of papers."

SYNONYMS: bundle, stack

punctual   (adj)   (ˈpən[k]-chə[-wə]l)

ORIGIN: Latin *punctus* (a point)

MEANING: Acting at an appointed or regular time

CONTEXT: "Mrs. Hall has a reputation for being *punctual*; she has been with the firm for more than ten years and has never arrived late for work."

SYNONYMS: prompt, timely

ANTONYM: late

OTHER FORMS: punctually (adv.), punctuality (n.)

A. Focus on Meaning

Match each word with its synonym by writing the proper letter in the blank.

1. sheaf _____
2. punctual _____
3. smirk _____
4. punctuality _____
5. haughty _____
6. picturesque _____

a) leer   b) promptness   c) snobbish   d) prompt   e) bundle   f) artistic

B. Words in Context

Supply the proper form of the most appropriate vocabulary word.

haughty	heritage	humble	knack	punctual	sheaf	smirk

1. "Wipe that _____ off your face!" demanded the angry supervisor. "I won't have workers laughing at me when I'm trying to show them what to do."

2. The private was so nervous that she dropped the _____ of papers as she entered the general's office.

3. My mother says that her _____ in arriving at work at nine o'clock each morning helped her get a promotion.

4. I hope my _____ for getting along with young children will help me get a job babysitting this summer.

5. If Larry were not so _____ and assumed a humbler attitude, he would make friends easier.

6. Coach Fitzgerald told Pat that she would have to be _____ for soccer practice or else run five laps as a penalty for failing to show up on time.

7. As the old song says, "Be it ever so _____, there's no place like home."

8. Patti claimed that she _____ her beautiful teeth from her mother, who has never had a cavity.

apprentice ▪ foul

apprentice	(n)	(ə-´prent-əs)
ORIGIN:	Latin *apprehendere* (to take hold of)	
MEANING:	A person who works for another in order to learn a trade	
CONTEXT:	"Susan wants to be a carpenter; therefore, she became an *apprentice* to Mr. Overton, the best carpenter and cabinetmaker in town. "	
SYNONYMS:	learner, novice, trainee	
OTHER FORM:	apprenticeship (n.)	

foul	(adj)	(faü[ə]l)
ORIGIN:	Old English *fū l* (rotten)	
MEANING:	Offensive to the senses, disgusting	
CONTEXT:	"Could that *foul* odor be coming from a broken sewer line?"	
SYNONYMS:	loathsome, filthy, dirty, polluted, shameful, vulgar, coarse, obscene	
ANTONYMS:	clean, pure, fragrant	
OTHER FORM:	foully (adv.)	

A. Focus on Meaning

Circle the letter of the best meaning for each vocabulary word.

1. apprentice: a) carpenter   b) learner   c) master thief   d) difficult concept

2. foul: a) inexperienced   b) disgusting   c) personal   d) harmful

3. apprenticeship: a) rank of seaman   b) assistant to the admiral
     c) time spent learning a trade   d) a passenger liner

4. sheaf: a) horizontal ledge   b) the husks from certain types of grain
     c) bundle   d) toddler

5. foul: a) filthy   b) redundant   c) reluctant   d) overbearing

6. picturesque: a) found only in an art gallery   b) quaint   c) pale   d) hard to see

B. Words in Context

Supply the proper form of the most appropriate vocabulary word.

apprentice	foul	hoard	layman	punctual	smirk

1. Henry learned to build solar-heating plants by being a(n) _____ to Mr. Miles, an expert in energy systems.

2. Pollutants had turned the stream so _____ that the fish were dying.

3. The foreign student's mispronunciation of several English words caused several students in the back of the room to _____ disrespectfully.

4. We could not go swimming in the _____, stagnant water.

5. Heather has served her _____ and is now a licensed plumber.

6. The fans were _____ for the concert, but the band was ten minutes late.

7. Rock climbing can be very dangerous and is not something a _____ should attempt alone.

8. When a blizzard was forecast, many people ran out to the supermarket to _____ milk and bread before the storm hit.

lesson 25
destiny ▪ allot

destiny (n) (ˈdes-tə-nē)

ORIGIN: Latin *destinare* (to determine)

MEANING: Something that is to happen to a particular person or thing in the future

CONTEXT: "The *destiny* of many families was determined by the skill of the captain and the crew of the *Mayflower* in reaching the new land."

SYNONYMS: fate, future, fortune

OTHER FORMS: destined (adj.), destine (v.), destination (n.)

allot (v) (ə-ˈlät)

ORIGIN: Latin *ad* (to, toward) + *lot* (lot)

MEANING: To assign as a portion or a share

CONTEXT: "Refugee families were *allotted* food according to the health and age of each family member."

SYNONYMS: apportion, assign, allocate

OTHER FORM: allotment (n.)

A. Focus on Meaning

Circle the letter of the word or phrase in each group that does not belong.

1. a) destiny   b) fate   c) future   d) desert
2. a) allot   b) assign   c) avow   d) apportion
3. a) apprentice   b) trainee   c) novice   d) painter
4. a) destination   b) goal   c) purpose   d) departure
5. a) foul   b) dirty   c) friendly   d) polluted
6. a) sheaf   b) stack   c) bundle   d) sheet

B. Words in Context

Supply the proper form of the most appropriate vocabulary word.

allot	destiny	punctual	sheaf

1. The _____ of our country depends on the decision its citizens make today.
2. When equipment was passed out, each team was _____ a specific number of bats, balls, and gloves.
3. When he was a child, George Washington had no idea that he was _____ to be the first President of the United States.
4. During World War II, each family was given a(n) _____ of gasoline, and only that portion could be bought.
5. If you are not _____, the school bus will leave without you.
6. A number of _____ of corn stalks form what is called a chock of corn.

C. Antonyms

Circle the letter of the word whose meaning is most nearly opposite the vocabulary word.

1. layman   a) amateur   b) specialist   c) artist   d) novice
2. magnitude   a) smallness   b) magnificence   c) immensity   c) sturdy
3. picturesque   a) quaint   b) artistic   c) plain   c) filthy
4. haughty   a) lordly   b) overbearing   c) funny   d) modes
5. humility   a) modesty   b) arrogance   c) cowardice   d) valor
6. punctual   a) timely   b) prompt   c) late   d) lazy

lesson 26

sub- ▪ super-

sub- (prefix)

ORIGIN: Latin *sub* (under, below)

MEANING: Under, beneath, below; to a lesser degree than, somewhat slightly; lower in rank or position

CONTEXT: "*sub*marine"

OTHER FORMS: sus- (suspend), sur- (surrender), suc- (succeed), sug- (suggest), sup- (supplant), suf- (suffice)

super- (prefix)

ORIGIN: Latin *super* (over, above, in addition to)

MEANING: Over, above, extra

CONTEXT: "*super*vise"

A. Focus on Meaning

In each of the italicized words below, underline the word part that you have learned. Then, using your knowledge of the meaning of the word part, circle the letter of the best meaning for the italicized word.

1. *subdivide* the land: a) divide into larger plots   b) divide into smaller plots
   c) improve by planting crops   d) sell to the highest bidder

2. *superlative* performance: a) entertaining   b) sloppy   c) musical   d) above average

3. *import* shoes: a) send out   b) hunt for   c) carry in   d) improve

4. *submerge* the bottle: a) fill with water   b) float   c) put under water   d) place on shelf

5. *export* wheat: a) bring into country   b) produce in country
   c) consume in country   d) send out of country

6. *supervision*:   a) visitation   b) practice   c) overseeing   d) ignoring

7. *subterranean* passages: a) on the surface of the earth   b) between the mountains
   c) built over a river   d) under the surface of the earth

B. REVIEW

Match the correct definition to each vocabulary word. Write the letter of the definition on the line.

_____ 1. foul   a. trainee

_____ 2. humility   b. bundle

_____ 3. punctual   c. filthy

_____ 4. repulse   d. meekness

_____ 5. apprentice   e. leer

_____ 6. smirk   f. prompt

_____ 7. hurtle   g. rush

_____ 8. sheaf   h. reject

lesson 27

vagabond ▪ dominate

vagabond (n) (ˈvag-ə-ˌbånd)

ORIGIN:	Latin *vagari* (to wander)
MEANING:	A person without a fixed home who wanders from place to place
CONTEXT:	"That fellow is a *vagabond*, roaming from town to town and begging for money to buy food."
SYNONYMS:	tramp, hobo, vagrant, wanderer, loafer
ANTONYMS:	settler, resident homeowner
OTHER FORMS:	vagabondish (adj.)

dominate (v) (ˈdåm-ə-ˌnāt)

ORIGIN:	Latin *dominus* (master)
MEANING:	To have controlling power, to rise above in order to rule
CONTEXT:	"After being elected mayor she refused to be *dominated* by her associates and continued to do what she considered best."
SYNONYMS:	control, rule, tower over, prevail
ANTONYMS:	follow, heed, submit
OTHER FORMS:	domination (n.)

A. Focus on Meaning

Circle the letter of the best meaning for each vocabulary word.

1. vagabond: a) wanderer   b) servant   c) homeowner   d) shortcut

2. dominate: a) serve   b) follow   c) control   d) defend

3. destiny: a) disguise   b) future   c) dominion   d) place

4. vagabondish: a) like a settler   b) like a wanderer   c) like a villain   d) like a resident

5. domination: a) control   b) attention   c) guidance   d) imitation

6. allot: a) serve   b) take away   c) collect   d) allocate

B. Words in Context

Supply the proper form of the most appropriate vocabulary word.

dominate	foul	knack	lateral	vagabond

1. Although most girls would resent _____ by an elder brother, Patricia seems to be quite content to let Rick make all her decisions for her.

2. _____ used to travel across the country by stowing away on freight trains, where they slept in empty boxcars.

3. Such a(n) _____ odor came from the cave that we decided some animal must be dead inside.

4. The old rooster _____ all the chickens; he "ruled the roost" in a grand manner.

5. In the winter many _____ escape the cold by traveling south for the season.

6. Lisa has a wonderful _____ of making a joke to relieve stress when people get nervous.

7. The lifeguard at the beach told us to swim _____ to the shore if we ever got caught in a riptide.

8. Our soccer coach told us that we had to _____ the play at midfield if we wanted to win the game.

lesson 28

persevere ▪ dormant

persevere (v) (ˌpər-sə-ˈvi[ə]r)		**dormant** (adj) (ˈdȯr-mənt)	
ORIGIN:	Latin *perseverus* (very strict)	ORIGIN:	Latin *dormire* (to sleep)
MEANING:	To keep at something in spite of obstacles or difficulties	MEANING:	In a state of rest or inactivity, appearing to be asleep
CONTEXT:	"That girl *persevered* and finished high school despite poverty and the indifference of her family."	CONTEXT:	"*Dormant* tulip bulbs that have lain in the ground all fall and winter send up foliage in the spring and begin to bloom in April."
SYNONYMS:	continue, persist, endure	SYNONYMS:	inactive, latent, quiescent, potential
ANTONYMS:	quit, give up	ANTONYMS:	active
OTHER FORM:	perseverance (n.)		

A. Focus on Meaning

Match each word with its synonym by writing the proper letter in the blank.

1. persevere____   2. dormant ____   3. vagabond ____

4. destiny ____   5. dominate ____   6. perseverance ____

a) wanderer   b) future   c) rule   d) persistence   e) continue   f) inactive

B. Words in Context

Supply the proper form of the most appropriate vocabulary word.

allot   destiny   dormant   persevere   vagabond

1. Seeds may lie _____ in the desert for several years until enough rain causes them to germinate.

2. Even in the face of harsh criticism, Frederick Douglass _____ in pressing for freedom for black people in the years just before the Civil War.

3. Young George Carver did not know that his _____ was to become a great scientist.

4. Deciduous trees become _____ in winter; their leaves wither and fall off.

5. Dr. Jonas Salk _____ in his search for a vaccine for polio until he succeeded.

6. In planning the new campground, officials _____ more space to each campsite than had been allocated in the old campground.

7. When I was a child on the farm, many _____ slept in our barn and were fed breakfast by my mother before they traveled on.

Shades of Meaning

- dormant
- latent
- quiescent
- potential

Dormant suggest in inactivity of something as though sleeping. *Latent* applies to a quality or power that has not come into sight or action but may at any time. *Quiescent* usually suggests a temporary stopping of activity. *Potential* applies to what as yet does not have being or effect but is soon likely to have.

lesson 29

distinctive ▪ edit

distinctive	(adj)	(dis-´ting[k]-tiv)		**edit**	(v)	(´ed-ət)
ORIGIN:	Latin *distinguere* (to distinguish)			ORIGIN:	Latin *edere* (to publish)	

distinctive (adj) (dis-´ting[k]-tiv)

ORIGIN: Latin *distinguere* (to distinguish)

MEANING: A quality that marks a person or a thing as being different from others

CONTEXT: "Her distinctive speech makes it clear, she grew up in another section of the country."

SYNONYMS: different, individual, unusual

ANTONYMS: indistinctive, typical, commonplace

OTHER FORMS: distinct (adj.), distinctiveness (n.), distinctively (adv.)

edit (v) (´ed-ət)

ORIGIN: Latin *edere* (to publish)

MEANING: To adapt and prepare (especially for publication) or to direct the publication of

CONTEXT: "I asked Paul to *edit* all material submitted so that it will be correct and suitable for use in the school paper."

SYNONYMS: adapt, alter, refine, correct

OTHER FORMS: edition (n.), editor (n.), editorial (n.), editorial (a j.)

A. Focus on Meaning

Circle the letter of the best meaning for each vocabulary word.

1. distinctive:　　a) individual　b) typical　c) discolored　d) relating to a district

2. edit:　　a) expose　b) adapt　c) bury　d) apply pressure to

3. persevere:　　a) puncture　b) place under arrest　c) persist　d) multiply

4. dormant:　　a) stubborn　b) audible　c) relating to doors　d) inactive

5. distinct:　　a) incorrect　b) having an unpleasant smell　c) different　d) haughty

6. edition:　　a) something published at one time　b) encyclopedia　c) lie　d) motor

B. Words in Context

Supply the proper form of the most appropriate vocabulary word.

edit	distinctive	dominate	hereditary	picturesque	swagger	vagabond

1. The _____ stripes of the zebra set it apart from other horselike animals.

2. _____ in newspapers express the opinions of their publishers.

3. The woman explained that her people had always been _____, traveling throughout Europe and taking whatever work they could find.

4. Too often, it seems, violence _____ the news, and more peaceful events are ignored.

5. "If you _____ this story," said Miss Townsend, "I think it may be appropriate for the literary magazine."

6. You can spot Louis from afar; his _____ walk is quite _____.

7. Pavlov was the first to describe the laws of _____.

8. Cades Cove, nestled in the Great Smoky Mountains, is one of the most _____ valleys I have ever seen.

lesson 30
cantankerous ▪ foliage

cantankerous (adj) (kan-ˈtang-k[ə-]rəs)

ORIGIN: Probably Middle English *contac* (strife) + *cankerous* (ulcerlike sore)

MEANING: Ill-natured, quarrelsome

CONTEXT: "Lucy is very pleasant, but her *cantankerous* older sister is quite the opposite."

SYNONYMS: irritable, peevish, grouchy

ANTONYMS: pleasant, good-natured

OTHER FORMS: cantankerousness (n.), cantankerously (adv.)

foliage (n) (ˈfō-l[ē]ij)

ORIGIN: Latin *follia* (leaves)

MEANING: Leaves of a plant

CONTEXT: "I wonder why the *foliage* of that elm tree has turned yellow, whereas the nearby elms remain green."

SYNONYM: leafage

OTHER FORMS: foliaged (adj.)

A. Focus on Meaning

Circle the letter of the best meaning for each vocabulary word.

1. cantankerous: a) pleasant   b) polite   c) ill-natured   d) haughty

2. foliage: a) bark   b) leafage   c) blooms   d) limbs

3. distinctive: a) loud   b) distant   c) different   d) unclear

4. cantankerous: a) good-natured   b) snobbish   c) irritable   d) quiet

5. edit: a) refine   b) compare   c) perform   d) read

6. foliage: a) leaves   b) fruit   c) stems   d) twigs

B. Words in Context

Supply the proper form of the most appropriate vocabulary word.

apprentice	cantankerous	dominant	dormant	foliage	haughty	persevere

1. In the fall the _____ of the trees turns many brilliant colors.

2. The clerk is a(n) _____ person who snaps at anyone who asks him a question.

3. When Gwen moved into an expensive neighborhood, she immediately took on an air of _____ that her sister considered very unbecoming to her.

4. Rose bushes do not die in winter but lie _____ until spring.

5. In Tennessee and Arkansas, the _____ of the sumac shrubs is the first to turn red in the fall.

6. Scrooge, in Dickens's *A Christmas Carol*, is a grouchy, _____ man before he is visited by a series of ghosts.

7. Every _____ must _____ if she or he ever hopes to become a master in her or his craft or trade.

8. Queen Victoria was one of the most _____ personalities in the nineteenth century.

Lesson 30 • CANTANKEROUS/FOLIAGE **35**

lesson 31

-ben- ▪ pro-

-ben-   (root)

ORIGIN: Latin *bene* (well)

MEANING: Good; favorable

CONTEXT: "*ben*evolent"

pro-   (prefix)

ORIGIN: Greek and Latin *pro* (before, forward, forth, for)

MEANING 1: Forward; before (both place and time)

CONTEXT 1: "*pro*peller"

MEANING 2: For, in favor of, supporting

CONTEXT 2: "*pro*-American"

A. Focus on Meaning

In each of the italicized words below, underline the word part that you have learned. Then, using your knowledge of the meaning of the word part, circle the letter of the best meaning for the italicized word.

1. *benefactor* of the hospital: a) one who receives   b) one who hinders
     c) one who does good for someone else   d) one who rules

2. *suppress* public opinion: a) talk about   b) influence
     c) report in a newspaper   d) hold down under tight control

3. the pope's *benediction*:   a) speech   b) appearance   c) blessing or good wishes
     d) religious robes used only on ceremonial occasions

4. *prospective* earnings: a) current   b) looked for in the future   c) not legal   d) poor

5. *superheat* the metal: a) heat again   b) lower the temperature
     c) heat for a long time   d) heat to very high temperature

6. *projection* of the cliff: a) height   b) steepness
     c) a part that juts forward   d) a part that recedes, goes back

B. REVIEW

Match the correct definition to each vocabulary word. Write the letter of the definition on the line.

_____ 1. distinctive   a. continue

_____ 2. imperative   b. different

_____ 3. persevere   c. necessary

_____ 4. cantankerous   d. control

_____ 5. dominate   e. grouchy

_____ 6. somber   f. wanderer

_____ 7. dormant   g. inactive

_____ 8. vagabond   h. depressing

lesson 32

stimulate ▪ prophesy

stimulate (v) (ˈstim-yə-ˌlāt)

ORIGIN: Latin *stimulare* (to goad)

MEANING: To arouse to action or effort by encouragement, pressure, or by a stimulant (such as tea, coffee, or a drug)

CONTEXT: "Rita's interest in public speaking was *stimulated* when she was chosen to represent her class in a speech contest."

SYNONYMS: activate, excite, goad, prod, incite, provoke

ANTONYMS: discourage, depress, deaden

OTHER FORMS: stimulant (n.), stimulator (n.), stimulative (adj.)

prophesy (v) (ˈpräf-ə-ˌsī)

ORIGIN: Greek *pro* (before) + *phanai* (to speak)

MEANING: To predict; to indicate or declare beforehand

CONTEXT: "Reverend Bennett of the Church of the Mystic Mind maintains that he can *prophesy* what will happen next year."

SYNONYMS: foretell, predict, forecast

OTHER FORMS: prophesier (n.), prophet (n.), prophecy (n.)

A. Focus on Meaning

Circle the letter of the best meaning for each vocabulary word.

1. stimulate: a) imitate   b) lull to sleep   c) activate   d) investigate

2. prophesy: a) protect   b) predict   c) protest   d) prod

3. cantankerous: a) jolly   b) grouchy   c) well   d) ill

4. stimulant: something that   a) arouses   b) pleases   c) confuses   d) saddens

5. prophet: person who   a) profits   b) foretells   c) protests   d) helps

B. Words in Context

Supply the proper form of the most appropriate vocabulary word.

edit   destiny   foliage   foul   prophesy   stimulate

1. I wish your classmates could _____ your interest in English as much as your teammates have aroused your interest in football.

2. To the alarm of conservationists, several acres of green _____ had already been destroyed by the Dutch elm beetle.

3. The fortune-teller's _____ that Ann would soon find money has led her to search trash cans.

4. All material submitted to a magazine is _____ before it is published.

5. Some people are so _____ by coffee that they do not drink it at night because it would keep them awake.

6. The oil spill _____ the beaches for miles and almost caused the beach resorts to close for two weeks.

7. There are those who believe that Nostrodamus _____ the twentieth-century _____ of European nations.

8. A field trip to the planetarium _____ the classes interest in astronomy.

lesson 33

profess ▪ bureaucracy

profess (v) (prə-ˈfes)

ORIGIN: Latin *protteri* (to avow publicly)

MEANING: To declare openly and freely; to affirm (sometimes in words or appearance only)

CONTEXT: "Mrs. Wright *professed* a belief in the cause and offered to help in any way she could."

SYNONYMS: acknowledge, avow, declare

OTHER FORMS: professed (adj.), professedly (adv.), profession (n.)

bureaucracy (n) (byü-ˈràk-rə-sē)

ORIGIN: Late Latin *burra* (rough cloth) + Greek *kratie* (rule, government)

MEANING: Excessive use of rules, regulations, and forms by administrative agencies

CONTEXT: "Because of the *bureaucracy* in our state government, it will be difficult to get a prompt hearing on the matter."

SYNONYMS: officialism, red tape

OTHER FORMS: bureau (n.), bureaucrat (n.), bureaucratic (adj.)

A. Focus on Meaning

Match each word with its synonym by writing the proper letter in the blank.

1. profess _____
2. bureaucracy _____
3. stimulate _____
4. profession _____
5. prophesy _____
6. bureau _____

a) excite   b) affirmation   c) officialism   d) foretell   e) agency   f) declare

B. Words in Context

Supply the proper form of the most appropriate vocabulary word.

| allot   bureaucracy   cantankerous   distinctive   edit   profess |

1. Mr. Stone _____ to have seen a UFO land in the vacant lot across from his home, but so far none of his neighbors has confirmed his observation.

2. Some government officials are mere _____ rather than true servants of the people.

3. That _____ pony tried to nip Mom's arm as she was saddling it.

4. George _____ to like sailing and agreed to crew for Penny just to be with her.

5. One of the _____ features of a children's hospital is the large number of playrooms to be found throughout the building.

6. The _____ in most countries makes it very difficult for people to bring problems to the attention of the government without going through miles of red tape.

7. I always try to _____ myself enough time to _____ my homework before I hand it in.

8. Although Scott _____ to like science, he failed to sign up for even one science course next year.

lesson 34
casual ▪ fiend

casual	(adj)	(ˈkazh-[ə]wəl)		**fiend**	(n)	(fēnd)

ORIGIN:	Latin *casus* (fall, chance)		ORIGIN:	Old English *fiend* (enemy)
MEANING:	Occurring by chance; with little or no concern being felt		MEANING:	An extremely wicked or cruel person
			CONTEXT:	"No one but a *fiend* could have treated a little child so cruelly."
CONTEXT:	"Although we were friendly when we were children, a *casual* conversation is all we ever have now."		SYNONYMS:	demon, devil
			OTHER FORMS:	fiendish (adj.), fiendishly (adv.)
SYNONYMS:	incidental, nonchalant, informal			
ANTONYMS:	planned, deliberate			
OTHER FORMS:	casually (adv.), casualness (n.)			

A. Focus on Meaning

Circle the letter of the best meaning for each vocabulary word.

1. casual: a) relating to checks   b) informal   c) incomplete   d) weak
2. fiendish: a) dealing with friends   b) statistical   c) dull   d) devilish
3. profess: a) declare   b) place oneself opposite   c) dress flashily   d) switch to
4. casually: a) stupidly   b) nonchalantly   c) strangely   d) fitfully
5. bureaucracy: a) sealing wax   b) carbonated beverage   c) underside of a leaf   d) red tape
6. fiend: a) demon   b) electronic equipment   c) soldier   d) fuse

B. Words in Context

Supply the proper form of the most appropriate vocabulary word.

casual	fiend	prophesy	stimulate

1. Paula's air of _____ after being asked for a date by Ben was a cover-up of her real feelings of surprise and excitement.
2. Chest massage is often used to _____ a heart that has stopped beating.
3. The _____ laughter of the cruel girl as she beat the dog aroused the anger of the neighbors.
4. _____ dress is appropriate for most social events at school.
5. Jeanne Dixon, a seer, _____ the death of President Kennedy at the hands of an assassin.
6. He becomes a(n) _____ under the influence of alcohol, often mistreating his family.

C. Antonyms

Circle the letter of the word whose meaning is most nearly opposite the vocabulary word.

1. foul   a) vulgar   b) course   c) gentle   d) clean
2. distinctive   a) commonplace   b) unusual   c) attractive   d) grim
3. dominate   a) control   b) follow   c) rule   d) focus
4. stimulate   a) activate   b) provoke   c) discourage   d) stop
5. persevere   a) continue   b) endure   c) give up   d) control
6. cantankerous   a) grouchy   b) deliberate   c) different   d) pleasant

lesson 35

ruddy ▪ avert

ruddy   (adj)   (´rəd-ē)

ORIGIN: Old English *rudu* (redness)

MEANING: Having a healthy reddish color

CONTEXT: "When I remarked on his *ruddy* complexion, he said he was sunburned."

SYNONYM: reddish

ANTONYM: pale

OTHER FORMS: ruddiness (n.)

avert   (v)   (ə-´vərt)

ORIGIN: Latin *avertere* (to turn away) ''

MEANING: To turn away, to prevent from happening

CONTEXT: "The driver *averted* an accident by pulling off the road."

SYNONYMS: prevent, ward off, turn aside

ANTONYM: cause

A. Focus on Meaning

Circle the letter of the best meaning for each vocabulary word.

1. ruddy: a) dirty   b) reddish   c) weak   d) strong

2. avert: a) turn upside down   b) encourage   c) turn away   d) increase

3. usual: a) planned   b) long   c) dead   d) informal

4. ruddy: a) healthy color   b) tired   c) fat   d) broken

5. avert: a) prevent   b) continue   c) cause   d) guess

6. fiend: a) companion   b) performer   c) distance   d) devil

B. Words in Context

Supply the proper form of the most appropriate vocabulary word.

avert	bureaucracy	casual	foliage	profess	stimulate	ruddy

1. By banking sharply to the left, the airline pilot _____ a crash with the light plane.

2. Although the invitations had specified _____ dress, Carole arrived at the party dressed in an elegant formal gown!

3. "Now that you've _____ sincere regret over forgetting to mail my letter at noon, why don't you rush out now and take it to the post office?" asked his mother.

4. When giving a talk, don't _____ your eyes but look directly at your audience.

5. My little sister, who was ill so long, is just now getting back her _____ coloring.

6. Because of the dry summer, the autumn _____ was not nearly as colorful as usual this year.

7. By taking a brisk walk every day one can _____ good health and a _____ complexion.

8. The mayor _____ a fight with the state _____ by withdrawing, for now, his plan to take over the city school system.

lesson 36

-sta- ▪ -dict-

-sta-	(root)		**-dict-**	(root)
ORIGIN:	Latin *stare* (to stand)		ORIGIN:	Latin *dictare* (to say)
MEANING:	To stand		MEANING:	Say, command, speak, word
CONTEXT:	"in*sta*nce"		CONTEXT:	"contra*dict*ion"
OTHER FORMS:	-stat- (status), -sist- (resist), -sti- (substitute)			

A. Focus on Meaning

In each of the italicized words below, underline the word parts that you have learned. Then, using your knowledge of the meanings of the word parts, circle the letter of the best meaning for the italicized word. (For some words there may be only one word part.)

1. increased in *stature*: a) wealth b) knowledge
   c) volume when speaking d) height when standing

2. give a *benediction*: a) spoken blessing b) condemnation c) benefit d) curse

3. *beneficent* woman: a) kindly b) beautiful c) wise d) intelligent

4. *static* opinions: a) strange b) standing still c) different d) changing

5. *contradict* a statement: a) support b) write c) speak against d) read

6. to *procrastinate* in doing one's homework: a) do now b) do in part
   c) put off until a future time d) forget to do

7. a *stationary* sign: a) movable b) not readable c) standing still d) road

8. *insist* on fairness: a) take a firm stand b) hope for c) work for d) ask for

9. *unhealthy* attitude: a) pleasant b)good c) desirable d) not desirable

B. REVIEW

Match the correct definition to each vocabulary word. Write the letter of the definition on the line.

_____ 1. casual   a. demon

_____ 2. profess   b. ward off

_____ 3. fiend   c. forecast

_____ 4. avert   d. pamper

_____ 5. indulge   e. informal

_____ 6. stimulate   f. dejected

_____ 7. melancholy   g. excite

_____ 8. prophesy   h. declare

lesson 37

via ▪ bestow

via   (prep)   ('vī-ə)

ORIGIN: Latin *via* (way)

MEANING: By way of a route; by way of an agency, medium, or instrumentality

CONTEXT: "I will go to Washington, D.C., *via* Eagle Airlines."

bestow   (v)   (bi-'stō)

ORIGIN: Middle English *bestowen* (to give)

MEANING: To present as a gift; give; confer

CONTEXT: "Because the child has always had so much attention *bestowed* on her, she has become very selfish."

SYNONYM: give, confer, donate, present

ANTONYM: receive

OTHER FORM: bestowal (n.)

A. Focus on Meaning

Circle the letter of the word or phrase in each group that does not belong.

1.   a) via   b) by way of a route   c) in the way   d) by way of an agency

2.   a) bestow   b) give   c) donate   d) receive

3.   a) ruddy   b) healthy color   c) pale   d) reddish

4.   a) avert   b) prevent   c) cause   d) ward off

5.   a) via   b) by train   c) by car   d) by the side of

6.   a) bestow   b) present   c) confer   d) take

B. Words in Context

Supply the proper form of the most appropriate vocabulary word.

> bestow   casual   fiend   via

1.   The _____ of the trophy is to take place during the assembly.

2.   We had planned to visit Moscow _____ London and Paris but were forced to fly direct by a hijacker who sought political asylum in the Soviet Union.

3.   Anita's _____ comment on the election showed she did not care who won.

4.   It is a shorter distance _____ the state highway, but that route takes more time than using Interstate 40.

5.   The kindly Dr. Jekyll was transformed by an experimental drug into a(n) _____ called Mr. Hyde, in Robert Louis Stevenson's tale of a split personality.

6.   Kindness and love _____ on a dog will usually make it your friend forever.

Shades of Meaning

- give
- bestow
- confer
- donate
- present

lesson 38

ally ▪ vibrate

ally (n) (´al-ī)

ORIGIN: Latin *ad* (to, toward) + *ligare* (to bind)

MEANING: One united or associated with another for some common purpose

CONTEXT: "In both world wars, the United States, France, and Britain were *allies*."

SYNONYM: supporter, helper, aide, associate

ANTONYMS: enemy, opponent

OTHER FORMS: allied (adj.), alliance (n.), ally (v.)

vibrate (v) (´vī-ˌbrāt)

ORIGIN: Latin *vibrare* (to shake)

MEANING: To move to and fro, from side to side, or up and down quickly and repeatedly, to quiver

CONTEXT: "Guitar strings *vibrate* and produce sound when plucked."

SYNONYMS: shake, quiver, oscillate, tremble, pulsate

OTHER FORMS: vibration (n.), vibrator (n.), vibrant (adj. meaning "pulsating with life")

A. Focus on Meaning

Circle the letter of the best meaning for each vocabulary word.

1. ally: a) officer   b) soldier   c) supporter   d) enemy

2. vibrate: a) tune   b) quiver   c) exhibit violent behavior   d) study science

3. via: a) hereby   b) therefore   c) by way of   d) around

4. ally: a) place in a prone position   b) unite   c) listen   d) cut off

5. bestow: a) store on lowest shelf   b) present to   c) hide   d) represent

B. Words in Context

Supply the proper form of the most appropriate vocabulary word.

ally	avert	bestow	distinctive	profess	vibrant

1. "You can depend on me as a(n) _____ in your campaign against water pollution," promised Sally.

2. When the front wheels of a car are out of line, the steering wheel may begin to _____.

3. Many church and civic organizations have _____ themselves with city governments in the struggle to end poverty.

4. The police hoped to _____ looting in the area by turning out in force before trouble began.

5. The _____ colors of the foliage in the fall are lively and stimulate the senses.

6. Easter lilies have a _____ aroma that fills any room in which they are placed.

7. Scott _____ his love for Angie on the first anniversary of their meeting.

8. College scholarships were _____ upon fifteen students from our class.

lesson 39

domestic ▪ teem

domestic   (adj)   (də-ˈməs-tik)

ORIGIN:	Latin *domus* (house)
MEANING:	Of or pertaining to the household, the family, one's own country; tame, not found in nature
CONTEXT:	"My Aunt Jane was a very *domestic* woman, devoting all her time to her home and family."
SYNONYMS:	homebred, internal, tame
ANTONYM:	foreign, external, wild
OTHER FORM:	domesticate (v.)

teem   (v)   (tēm)

ORIGIN:	Old English *timan* (to bring forth)
MEANING:	To abound in or to fill to overflowing
CONTEXT:	"Because those lakes *teem* with fish, they are a paradise for people who enjoy fishing."
SYNONYMS:	abound, swarm, crowd
ANTONYM:	lack

A. Focus on Meaning

Circle the letter of the best meaning for each vocabulary word.

1. domestic: a) dome-shaped   b) tame   c) meat-eating   d) feasible

2. teem: a) form a group to work together   b) abound   c) bandage   d) please

3. ally: a) neon sign   b) false statement   c) supporter   d) column

4. domesticate: a) capture   b) confine   c) make tame   d) refuse

5. vibrate: a) accelerate   b) tremble   c) invest   d) observe

6. teeming: a) spoiling   b) weaving   c) swarming   d) decreasing

B. Words in Context

Supply the proper form of the most appropriate vocabulary word.

bestow   casual   domestic   fiend   teem

1. The Lapps have _____ the reindeer to the extent that the animals can be milked, ridden, and herded like cattle.

2. The small lakes created under a system of flood control were well stocked by the state Game and Fish Commission and now _____ with fish.

3. A great honor was _____ on my father when he was named a Master Farmer of Oklahoma.

4. During the hunting season, hunters should have no trouble getting their limit of squirrels because the woods are _____ with them.

5. For the prom the dress code is formal; _____ clothes will not do.

6. America's favorite pet, the dog, was _____ by humans thousands of years ago.

7. When Dr. Frankenstein created the monster, was he a _____ or simply a misguided genius? There are at least two sides to the argument.

inter- ▪ intra-

inter- (prefix)

ORIGIN: Latin *inter* (under, in)

MEANING: Between, among

CONTEXT: "*inter*action"

intra- (prefix)

ORIGIN: Latin *intro* (within)

MEANING: Within, during

CONTEXT: "*intra*mural"

OTHER FORM: intro- (introvert)

A. Focus on Meaning

In each of the italicized words below, underline the word part that you have learned. Then, using your knowledge of the meaning of the word part, circle the letter of the best meaning for the italicized word.

1. *intramural* games: a) between two schools   b) within one school
   c) World Series   d) the Olympics

2. *intermittent* sounds: a) continual   b) loud   c) interesting   d) silence between

3. *status* in the Senate: a) leader   b) lowest rank   c) standing position   d) term

4. behavior of an *introvert*: a) outgoing person   b) intellectual person
   c) withdrawn person   d) happy person

5. *edict* of the queen: a) information   b) election   c) respect   d) command

6. *interpose* her opinion: a) withdraw   b) inject among   c) uphold   d) withhold

7. *prologue* of the novel: a) climax   b) introduction   c) ending   d) main character

8. *intravenous* treatment: a) outside the veins   b) within the veins
   c) drawing blood   d) life-saving

B. REVIEW

Match the correct definition to each vocabulary word. Write the letter of the definition on the line.

_____ 1. merge   a. supporter

_____ 2. ally   b. cower

_____ 3. via   c. give

_____ 4. version   d. blend

_____ 5. vibrate   e. postponement

_____ 6. cringe   f. by way of

_____ 7. bestow   g. story

_____ 8. suspension   h. shake

LESSONS 21–40

For each numbered word choose the word or phrase that is closest to the meaning of the vocabulary word. Write the letter for the word on the line provided.

1. picturesque   a) plain   b) quaint   1. _____
                  c) ugly   d) perfect

2. avert   a) cause   b) swerve   2. _____
                  c) divert   d) prevent

3. allot   a) borrow   b) rule   3. _____
                  c) allocate   d) locate

4. stimulate   a) discourage   b) imitate   4. _____
                  c) activate   d) donate

5. punctual   a) prompt   b) late   5. _____
                  c) vulgar   d) annual

6. persevere   a) give up   b) persist   6. _____
                  c) quit   d) prolong

7. profess   a) adapt   b) endure   7. _____
                  c) acknowledge   d) propose

8. casual   a) deliberate   b) planned   8. _____
                  c) carefree   d) informal

9. foul   a) pure   b) polluted   9. _____
                  c) fragrant   d) full

10. vibrate   a) change   b) continue   10. _____
                   c) shake   d) swarm

11. dominate   a) follow   b) submit   11. _____
                   c) pulsate   d) control

12. distinctive   a) commonplace   b) unusual   12. _____
                   c) typical   d) vulgar

13. cantankerous   a) irritable   b) pleasant   13. _____

                       c) good natured   d) abusive

14. bestow   a) receive   b) present   14. _____

                  c) stack   d) predict

15. domestic   a) foreign   b) wild   15. _____

                  c) homebred   d) different

16. ally   a) enemy   b) wanderer   16. _____

           c) trainee   d) supporter

17. dormant   a) active   b) dirty   17. _____

               c) inactive   d) graphic

18. smirk   a) bundle   b) leer   18. _____

           c) continue   d) insult

19. apprentice   a) novice   b) resident   19. _____

                c) helper   d) aide

20. vagabond   a) bureaucrat   b) prophet   20. _____

               c) wanderer   d) trainee

Test Tips

As you have seen, a synonym test asks you to choose a synonym for the word being tested. In an attempt to confuse you, sometimes test makers may include and antonym or two in the answers. Sometimes the answers may also include words with spellings or sounds similar to the correct word.

Practice: In each sentence choose the synonym for the italicized word. Write your answer on the line.

1. Closed up for months, the air was *foul* in the old mansion.   1. _____

    (a) polluted   (b) fragrant   (c) pure   (d) still

2. Risa *edited* her essay three times before she was satisfied with it.   2. _____

    (a) wrote   (b) shared   (c) tore up   (d) corrected

3. How is it that Stan is so *ruddy* when his sister, Jan, is so fair?   3. _____

    (a) pale   (b) lively   (c) reddish   (d) tanned

4. Two weeks after the huge rain storm Houston was *teeming* with mosquitoes.   4. _____

    (a) lacking   (b) searching for   (c) swarming   (d) spraying for

lesson 41

render ▪ attire

render	(v)	(ˈren-dər)
ORIGIN:	Latin *reddere* (to restore)	
MEANING:	To perform, furnish, provide	
CONTEXT:	"You *render* a great service when you give blood to the bloodbank."	
SYNONYMS:	furnish, supply, perform, express, deliver, fulfill	
OTHER FORM:	rendition (n.)	

attire	(n)	(ə-ˈtī[ə]r)
ORIGIN:	Old French *a* (to, toward) + *tire* (order, rank)	
MEANING:	Clothes or apparel, especially garments that are splendid and rich	
CONTEXT:	"The *attire* of the queen's guard dazzled the peasants who were clad in rags."	
SYNONYMS:	clothes, garb, raiment, dress, costume	
OTHER FORMS:	attire (v.), attired (adj.)	

A. Focus on Meaning

Circle the letter of the word or phrase in each group that does not belong.

1. a) take   b) furnish   c) render   d) perform

2. a) attire   b) dress   c) costume   d) Halloween

3. a) domestic   b) tame   c) homebred   d) international

4. a) render   b) perform   c) provide   d) profess

5. a) teem   b) laugh   c) swarm   d) abound

B. Words in Context

Supply the proper form of the most appropriate vocabulary word.

ally attire avert render teem via vibrate

1. The church choir's _____ of the anthem, "The Holy City," was excellent.

2. The salesperson demonstrated a new washing machine that uses ultrasonic _____ in place of the traditional agitator to shake loose dirt from laundry.

3. All the scouts were _____ in their uniforms for the parade.

4. Agnes Weston, by offering both legal and financial support for our activities, has been a powerful _____ in our struggle for civil rights.

5. Peace Corps volunteers are rewarded with satisfaction, not money, for the service they to _____ others.

6. Jeans and a sweatshirt are not suitable _____ for tonight's school dance.

7. By driving home _____ the longer valley road, we _____ the snowstorm in the mountains.

8. The rain, which _____ all night, caused many small streams to overflow their banks by morning.

lesson 42

awe ▪ penetrate

awe   (n)   (ȯ)

ORIGIN: Old Norse *agi* (terror, fear)

MEANING: An overpowering feeling of admiration, fear, or reverence caused by that which is grand or extremely powerful

CONTEXT: "We watched in *awe* as the huge new airplane lifted majestically off the runway."

SYNONYMS: reverence, veneration, fear

OTHER FORMS: awful (adj.), awfully (adv.)

penetrate   (v)   (ˈpen-ə-ˌtrāt)

ORIGIN: Latin *penetrare* (to pierce)

MEANING: To see into or through, to pass into or through, to enter

CONTEXT: "The bullet *penetrated* the thick wall about three inches above the boy's head."

SYNONYMS: pierce, perforate, invade, bore, enter, permeate

OTHER FORMS: impenetrable (adj.), penetrable (adj.)

A. Focus on Meaning

Circle the letter of the best meaning for each vocabulary word.

1. awe: a) indifference   b) reverence   c) expression of disgust   d) love

2. penetrate: a) pierce   b) praise   c) protect   d) electrocute

3. render: a) give   b) surrender   c) attract   d) overload

4. penetrate: a) invade   b) pant   c) warn   d) project

5. attire: a) customer   b) receipt   c) kit   d) costume

B. Words in Context

Supply the proper form of the most appropriate vocabulary word.

ally   awe   domestic   penetrate   teem

1. In parts of the Great Smoky Mountains, the forests are so thick that they are almost _____.

2. The prairies _____ with buffalo before the European settlers so wantonly slaughtered them.

3. Is it fair to import foreign-made goods that can be sold for less than _____ goods of the same quality?

4. The color, the barrenness, and the magnitude of the Painted Desert of north central Arizona filled me with _____.

5. Parking lights will barely _____ a mist at twilight; therefore, it is safer to turn on your headlights.

6. The fireworks display in New York harbor on July 4th is always one of the most _____ displays you will see anywhere.

7. More than fifty years ago, the United States and South Korea formed an _____ to defend South Korea from an invasion by North Korea.

lesson 43

tempest ▪ ascribe

tempest   (n)   (ˈtem-pəst)

ORIGIN: Latin *tempus* (time)

MEANING: A violent wind or storm; a violent commotion or tumult

CONTEXT: "When the *tempest* struck, we rushed to close the windows, hoping they would not be broken by the huge hailstones.

SYNONYMS: gale, disturbance, squall, tumult, turmoil

ANTONYM: tranquillity

OTHER FORMS: tempestuous (adj.), tempestuously (adv.)

ascribe   (v)   (ə-ˈskrīb)

ORIGIN: Latin *ascribere* (to attribute)

MEANING: To refer to or credit as coming from or belonging to a specific source or cause

CONTEXT: "The alphabet of the Cherokees is *ascribed* to Sequoyah. "

SYNONYMS: attribute, credit, assign

OTHER FORM: ascription (n.)

A. Focus on Meaning

Circle the letter of the best meaning for each vocabulary word.

1. tempest: a) surf   b) wave   c) storm   d) noise

2. ascribe: a) scribble   b) attribute   c) subscribe   d) write

3. awe: a) puzzlement   b) majesty   c) veneration   d) beauty

4. penetrate: a) slice   b) pierce   c) strain   d) chip

5. tempest: a) tumult   b) calm   c) pest   d) tormentor

6. ascribe: a) copy   b) agree   c) debit   d) assign

B. Words in Context

Supply the proper form of the most appropriate vocabulary word.

	attire	ascribe	render	tempest

1. The first time I heard the _____ ocean, I was sure a storm was raging.

2. "Jogging _____ is not suitable for this restaurant," the manager told a group of a hungry customers.

3. A nuclear accident at White Sands Proving Ground was _____ to the careless handling of plutonium explosives by two army technicians.

4. A verdict of guilty was _____ by the jury.

5. The discovery of gunpowder is _____ to the Chinese.

6. When the Secretary of the Army revealed that some West Point cadets had cheated on examinations, a(n) _____ erupted in Congress.

C. Antonyms

Circle the letter of the word whose meaning is most nearly opposite the vocabulary word.

1. casual   a) informal   b) nonchalant   c) deliberate   d) ruddy

2. avert   a) turn aside   b) cause   c) prevent   d) prod

3. ally   a) associate   b) helper   c) tramp   d) enemy

4. bestow   a) donate   b) receive   c) present   d) exchange

5. domestic   a) foreign   b) home bred   c) tame   d) awesome

6. ruddy   a) reddish   b) pale   c) weld   d) cloudy

lesson 44

-mit- ▪ -ject-

-mit-	(root)		**-ject-**	(root)
ORIGIN:	Latin *mittere* (to send)		ORIGIN:	Latin *jacere* (to throw)
MEANING:	To send		MEANING:	Throw
CONTEXT:	"trans*mit*"		CONTEXT:	"e*ject*"
OTHER FORMS:	-mitt- (intermittent), -miss- (transmission)			

A. Focus on Meaning

In each of the italicized words below, underline the word parts that you have learned. Then, using your knowledge of the meanings of the word parts, circle the letter of the best meaning for the italicized word. (For some words there may be only one word part.)

1. *remit* the money: a) remember   b) collect   c) send back   d) change

2. feel *dejected*: a) determined   b) cast down in spirits   c) proud   d) weird

3. *intermediary* agency: a) outside   b) go-between   c) inside   d) regulatory

4. *submit* a letter: a) to send   b) to throw away   c) to sign   d) to read

5. *subjected* to mistreatment: a) sent away or removed from   b) "cast down" or depressed about   c) thrown under or caused to undergo   d) stood up to or rejected

6. *intramuscular* tear: a) within a muscle   b) outside a muscle   c) between muscles   d) extra muscle

7. *indict* the woman: a) put in jail   b) give encouragement to   c) collect taxes from   d) accuse of or charge with committing a crime

8. *emit* light: a) absorb   b) dim   c) send out   d) block

9. hit by a *missile*: a) club   b) object thrown into space   c) profound idea   d) enemy

B. REVIEW

Match the correct definition to each vocabulary word. Write the letter of the definition on the line.

_____ 1. penetrate   a. credit

_____ 2. merge   b. raw-boned

_____ 3. awe   c. pierce

_____ 4. render   d. courage

_____ 5. attire   e. supply

_____ 6. gaunt   f. reverence

_____ 7. ascribe   g. unite

_____ 8. valor   h. clothes

lesson 45

covet ▪ zealous

covet (v) (ˈkəv-ət)

ORIGIN: Latin *cupere* (to desire)

MEANING: To wish for or desire another's possessions or to wish for something enviously

CONTEXT: "Mr. Swindle *covets* his neighbor's farm and will try any means, fair or unfair, to get it."

SYNONYMS: envy, crave, begrudge, desire

ANTONYM: covetous (adj.), covetously (adv.)

zealous (adj) (ˈzel-əs)

ORIGIN: Greek *zelos* (zeal)

MEANING: Extremely devoted to or active or diligent in the pursuit of something

CONTEXT: "Mrs. Rivera is a *zealous* supporter of the tax increase to be used for schools and is working diligently to persuade people to vote it."

SYNONYMS: passionate, enthusiastic, eager

ANTONYM: indifferent, apathetic

OTHER FORMS: zealously (adv.), zeal (n.), zealot (n.)

A. Focus on Meaning

Match each word with its synonym by writing the proper letter in the blank.

1. covet ____   2. zealous ____   3. tempest ____

4. covetous ____   5. ascribe ____   6. zeal ____

a) eagerness   b) desire   c) envious   d) credit   e) enthusiastic   f) disturbance

B. Words in Context

Supply the proper form of the most appropriate vocabulary word.

awe   covet   penetrate   zealous

1. The local Boy Scout troop began the 20-mile hike with great enthusiasm, but by the time the scouts reached the halfway mark, they had lost much of their _____ and trudged wearily onward.

2. If the rusty wire _____ your skin, you must have a tetanus shot at once.

3. Most students are in _____ of the principal, knowing how important she is.

4. The _____ Girl Scouts arrived early, eager to help convert the vacant lot into a playground for poor children.

5. Jim's _____ attitude keeps him unhappy, for he desires everything his friends have.

6. To _____ a good grade is not enough; one must work for it.

Shades of Meaning
- zealous
- passionate
- enthusiastic
- eager

Zealous implies being filled with energetic and relentless pursuit of a goal or devotion to a call. *Passionate* implies being filled with an emotion that is deeply stirring and uncontrollable. *Enthusiastic* applies to being filled with a lively or eager interest in or admiration for a proposal, cause, or activity. *Eager* implies passion and enthusiasm and sometimes impatience at delay or restraint.

lesson 46

cope ▪ reliable

cope	(v)	(kōp)
ORIGIN:	Middle French *couper* (to strike)	
MEANING:	To struggle, combat, or overcome, usually on even terms or with success, in order to overcome problems	
CONTEXT:	"After losing sight in both eyes, Kevin made a remarkable effort to *cope* with his handicap and lead a productive life."	
SYNONYMS:	contend, struggle, live with	

reliable	(adj)	(ri-ˈlī-ə-bəl)
ORIGIN:	Latin *religare* (to tie back)	
MEANING:	Fit to be depended upon	
CONTEXT:	"I have always found Fanny to be *reliable*; I am sure that you can depend on her to do what she says."	
SYNONYMS:	trustworthy, responsible, dependable	
ANTONYMS:	unreliable, irresponsible, undependable	
OTHER FORMS:	reliability (n.), reliableness (n.), reliably (adv.), reliance (n.), rely (v.)	

A. Focus on Meaning

Circle the letter of the best meaning for each vocabulary word.

1. cope: a) count   b) copy   c) struggle   d) destroy

2. reliable: a) resistible   b) dependable   c) defensible   d) able

3. covet: a) cover   b) take   c) desire   d) disregard

4. reliable: a) trustworthy   b) reluctant   c) irresponsible   d) patient

5. cope: a) contend   b) capture   c) ignore   d) understand

B. Words in Context

Supply the proper form of the most appropriate vocabulary word.

ascribe   attire   awe   cope   penetrate   reliable   render   tempest

1. The president _____ with a multitude of problems, both large and small, every day.

2. There was a time when some of Shakespeare's plays were _____ to other writers by researchers in literary history.

3. Mr. Jackson's continual _____ on artificial stimulants has led him to physical dependence on coffee.

4. Several members of the crew as well as a fishing vessel were lost in the recent _____ off the coast of Maine.

5. We have found the mechanics at Dependable Auto Service to be _____ workers.

6. We are frequently in _____ at the strange _____ that Ted wears to school some days.

7. Jesus said, "_____ unto Caesar the things that are Caesar's and to God the things that are God's."

8. In the second half the New York Knicks finally _____ with the way the Miami Heat had been easily _____ to the basket in the first half.

lesson 47

anecdote ▪ antidote

anecdote (n) (ˈan-ik-ˌdōt)	**antidote** (n) (ˈant-i-ˌdōt)
ORIGIN: Greek *anekdotos* (unpublished items)	ORIGIN: Greek *anti* (against) + *dotus* (given)
MEANING: A short narrative about an interesting or amusing incident	MEANING: Something that counteracts the effects of poison, disease, or injury
CONTEXT: "She wrote an *anecdote* about her most embarrassing moment."	CONTEXT: "Hard work is often an *antidote* to worry because it takes your mind off your troubles. "
SYNONYMS: sketch, tale, vignette	SYNONYMS: remedy, cure, relief
OTHER FORMS: anecdotal (adj.), anecdotist (n)	OTHER FORMS: antidotal (adj.), antidotally (adv.)

A. Focus on Meaning

Circle the letter of the best meaning for each vocabulary word.

1. anecdote: a) antibiotic   b) cure   c) short narrative   d) anger

2. antidote: a) antecedent   b) sketch   c) remedy   d) ancestor

3. cope: a) contend   b) extend   c) argue   d) influence

4. reliable: a) allowable   b) responsive   c) dependable   d) efficient

5. anecdote: a) poem   b) puzzle   c) answer   d) tale

6. antidote: a) sketch   b) cure   c) garb   d) vitamin

B. Words in Context

Supply the proper form of the most appropriate vocabulary word.

anecdote   antidote   covet   lateral   via   zealous

1. A number of interesting _____ have been written about Abe Lincoln.

2. In pioneer days, a tea made of the tansy plant was a(n) _____ for snakebite.

3. Trying to keep warm during the winter in those ice-covered shacks by the railroad must cause the miserable people there to _____ our snug homes.

4. You can fly to Paris _____ London if you wish.

5. From a(n) _____ view the monument is not distinctive, but from the front it is impressive.

6. Terry's mother is a(n) _____ supporter of civil rights; she devotes many hours and much energy to this cause.

7. Doctors and other health professionals say that there is strong evidence that regular physical exercise is a good _____ for stress.

8. On her last birthday my grandmother presented the family with several notebooks filled with her _____ about growing up on a farm in Iowa.

lesson 48

exploit ▪ query

exploit	(v)	(ik-ˊsploit)

ORIGIN: Latin *explicare* (to unfold)

MEANING: To make use of, to take advantage of, to utilize unfairly or for profit

CONTEXT: "Before child labor laws were passed, children were often *exploited* as a source of cheap labor."

SYNONYMS: utilize, abuse, mistreat, manipulate

OTHER FORMS: exploitable (adj.), exploit (n. meaning "daring deed"), exploitation (n.)

query	(n)	(ˊkwi[ə]r-ē)

ORIGIN: Latin *quaerere* (to ask)

MEANING: A question or inquiry

CONTEXT: "Mother did not know the reason for the FBI's *query* about our neighbor's daughter, but she answered all the questions the agents asked."

SYNONYMS: question, inquiry, doubt

OTHER FORM: query (v.)

A. Focus on Meaning

Circle the letter of the word in each group that does not belong.

1. a) exploit   b) explore   c) abuse   d) misapply

2. a) query   b) question   c) inquiry   d) assumption

3. a) anecdote   b) tale   c) remedy   d) sketch

4. a) exploitation   b) abuse   c) exploration   d) manipulation

5. a) antidote   b) antecedent   c) remedy   d) cure

6. a) query   b) doubt   c) inquire   d) believe

B. Words in Context

Supply the proper form of the most appropriate vocabulary word.

anecdote   ascribe   cope   exploit   query   reliable   zealous

1. The government has tried to curb the _____ of our natural resources by enacting conservation laws.

2. Mark became extremely nervous when his math teacher did not immediately answer his _____ about how he had done on the final exam.

3. Dad calls his 1972 car "Old _____" because it starts no matter how cold the day.

4. Grandfather never seems to tire of telling of his _____ as a miner and trapper in the West.

5. She sent a(n) _____ to local newspapers, asking whether they would be interested in a series of articles on her recent trip to Alaska.

6. To be successful in any competitive sport, you must _____ practice, practice, practice.

7. Martha _____ the _____ about working on a Mississippi River boat to her uncle Jake, but Mary insisted that they were written by their uncle Lou.

8. Cindy asked Claire, "Can I _____ on you to _____ with the twins for two hours while I go to the mall?"

lesson 49

-cap- ▪ -duct-

-cap-	(root)		**-duct-**	(root)
ORIGIN:	Latin *capere* (to take or seize)		ORIGIN:	Latin *ducere* (to lead)
MEANING:	Take		MEANING:	Lead
CONTEXT:	"*cap*ture"		CONTEXT:	"in*duct*ion"
OTHER FORMS:	-cep- (deception), -cept- (intercept), -cip- (incipient)		OTHER FORMS:	-duce- (reduce), -ducat- (educate), -due- (conducive)

A. Focus on Meaning

In each of the italicized words below, underline the word parts that you have learned. Then, using your knowledge of the meanings of the word parts, circle the letter of the best meaning for the italicized word. (For some words there may be only one word part.)

1. the criminal's *captor*: a) lawyer b) one who frees another c) one who takes another into custody d) a captain

2. *seduced* by a special sale: a) fooled b) led to buy c) discouraged from buying d) disappointed

3. given a favorable *reception*: a) grade on a test b) manner in which something is taken or accepted c) answer to a letter d) set of orders

4. *conducive* to success: a) harmful b) leading to or promoting c) addicted d) devoted

5. *remit* the correct amount: a) arrive at b) forget c) send back d) ask for

6. a *ductile* child: a) hard to control b) intelligent c) bored with school d) easily led

7. *interject* an idea: a) think of b) develop c) put in d) discover

8. *capable* worker: a) untrained b) tireless c) holding necessary skills d) lazy

B. REVIEW

Match the correct definition to each vocabulary word. Write the letter for the definition on the line.

_____ 1. covet   a. remedy

_____ 2. antidote   b. dreadful

_____ 3. cope   c. trustworthy

_____ 4. bureaucracy   d. red tape

_____ 5. zealous   e. tale

_____ 6. anecdote   f. envy

_____ 7. grim   g. live with

_____ 8. reliable   h. enthusiastic

lesson 50

assail ▪ quest

assail	(v)	(ə-ˈsā[ə]l)		quest	(n)	(kwest)

ORIGIN:	Latin *assilire* (to leap on)
MEANING:	To attack violently with arguments, ridicule, abuse, and often with blows
CONTEXT:	"When the candidate began to *assail* her opponent with ridicule and slander, I decided to leave the meeting."
SYNONYMS:	attack, malign, assault
OTHER FORM:	assailant (n.)

ORIGIN:	Latin *quaerere* (to seek)
MEANING:	An act of seeking to find or obtain something
CONTEXT:	"The UN's *quest* for a settlement of the Arab-Israeli problem has been unsuccessful so far."
SYNONYMS:	search, pursuit, hunt, mission
OTHER FORMS:	quester (n.), inquest (n.)

A. Focus on Meaning

Match each word with its synonym by writing the proper letter in the blank.

1. assail _____
2. quest _____
3. exploit _____
4. assailant _____
5. query _____
6. quester _____

a) use   b) assault   c) hunter   d) question   e) search   f) attacker

B. Words in Context

Supply the proper form of the most appropriate vocabulary word.

assail	covet	exploit	indulge	quest	query

1. In the dark Larry was unable to identify his _____.

2. Napoleon's _____ of even greater power led him to overextend his troops, which contributed to his ultimate downfall.

3. The mayor _____ his position in the community for his own financial gain.

4. My _____ to the Chamber of Commerce about summer jobs for teenagers has not been answered.

5. When the ambassador left the meeting, he was _____ by reporters who demanded that he tell them what had happened.

6. The old prospector never abandoned his _____ for minerals although he rarely struck a worthwhile vein.

7. Dr. Richardson (yielded to) _____ her taste for fine clothes in such a lavish fashion that her wardrobe became the envy of her colleagues.

8. In "A Modest Proposal," Jonathan Swift, the author of *Gulliver's Travels*, _____ the English policy toward the Irish.

lesson 51

jaunty ▪ chasm

jaunty   (adj)   (ˈjȯnt-ē)

ORIGIN: French *gentil* (noble, genteel)

MEANING: Lively in appearance and manner

CONTEXT: "The well-dressed elderly man, swinging a cane, walked through the park with a *jaunty* step."

SYNONYMS: lively, lighthearted

OTHER FORMS: jauntily (adv.), jauntiness (n.)

chasm   (n)   (ˈkaz-əm)

ORIGIN: Greek *chasma* (yawning hollow, gulf)

MEANING: A deep fissure or gorge in the Earth's surface

CONTEXT: "The scouting party, finding no way to cross the wide *chasm*, routed the wagon train around it to the north."

SYNONYMS: abyss, ravine, cleft, gulf, canyon, rift

A. Focus on Meaning

Circle the letter of the word in each group that does not belong.

1. a) chasm   b) abyss   c) cliff   d) gorge

2. a) assail   b) unfurl   c) attack   d) malign

3. a) quest   b) search   c) rebel   d) pursuit

4. a) jaunty   b) cheerful   c) lively   d) dangerous

5. a) chasm   b) rift   c) distance   d) canyon

B. Words in Context

Supply the proper form for the most appropriate vocabulary word.

chasm   exploit   gaunt   jaunty

1. Although frowned on by the more conservative members of the military establishment, President Kennedy approved the _____ headgear of the Green Berets, saying that it symbolized the fighting spirit of the U. S. Special Forces.

2. To the southwest of Colorado Springs is the Royal Gorge, a narrow _____ with sheer granite walls rising on each side to a great height.

3. Nancy, you _____ your friends by expecting them to wash your car and buy gas in exchange for letting them ride to the game with you.

4. The _____, drawn expressions on the faces of the rescue team said far more than words about what they had been through.

5. The _____ air and plumage of the blue jay always remind me of a lively woman.

6. The Hudson Canyon is a deep, underwater _____ in the Atlantic Ocean just east of New York City.

lesson 52
arid ▪ enlighten

arid   (adj)   (ˈar-əd)

ORIGIN: Latin *arere* (to be dry)

MEANING: Having insufficient rainfall to support agriculture; excessively dry

CONTEXT: "The *arid* land of central and southern California will produce bountiful crops if it is well irrigated."

SYNONYMS: dry, parched, waterless

ANTONYMS: moist, wet

OTHER FORMS: aridness (n.), aridity (n.)

enlighten   (v)   (in-ˈlīt-n)

ORIGIN: Old English *en* (in, into) + *leoht* (light)

MEANING: Instruct; impart knowledge to

CONTEXT: "Her lecture should *enlighten* me about the Navajo; I know so little about them."

SYNONYMS: teach, inform, educate

OTHER FORM: enlightenment (n.)

A. Focus on Meaning

Circle the letter of the best meaning for each vocabulary word.

1. arid: a) airy   b) dry   c) cold   d) drafty

2. enlighten: a) inform   b) reduce   c) lift   d) deduct

3. jaunty: a) fast   b) polished   c) lively   d) horrible

4. chasm: a) ravine   b) difficulty   c) ditch   d) hole

5. arid: a) irrigated   b) aired out   c) wet   d) waterless

6. enlightenment: a) education   b) enlistment   c) induction   d) entertainment

B. Words in Context

Supply the proper form of the most appropriate vocabulary word.

arid   chasm   covet   enlighten   jaunty

1. Israeli methods of irrigation provide an excellent example of how _____ land can be made into excellent farmland.

2. Television has helped _____ the public on many issues.

3. Mr. Smith is a senior citizen whose _____ step and fashionable attire suggest that he is young in spirit.

4. At Fall Creek Falls State Park visitors are no longer permitted to go down into the _____ by way of the steep cliff but must follow the long but less dangerous trail.

5. Will the increased _____ we gain be worth the tremendous amount of money and energy spent to establish the space station?

6. Some people are so allergic to bee stings that they must carry an _____ with them at all times.

7. There is a desert in Chile that is the most _____ place on Earth.

8. It is much better to work hard toward your goals rather than waste time and energy _____ one's neighbor's success.

lesson 53

foster ▪ reservoir

foster　(v)　('fȯs-tər)

ORIGIN:　Old English *fostor* (food)

MEANING:　To encourage, to promote the growth and the development of

CONTEXT:　"Joint meetings of civic clubs, churches, and businesses *foster* community development and cooperation."

SYNONYMS:　nurture, advance, instigate, nourish

ANTONYMS:　discourage, neglect

OTHER FORMS:　fosterer (n.)

reservoir　(n)　('rez-ə[r]v-ˌwȧr)

ORIGIN:　Middle French *reserver* (to reserve) + *oir* (a place)

MEANING:　A place where something is kept

CONTEXT:　"The dam on Skeleton River will create a large *reservoir* of water for ordinary as well as recreational use."

SYNONYMS:　store, supply, reserve

A. Focus on Meaning

Circle the letter of the best meaning for each vocabulary word.

1. foster:　　a) become apparent　b) exclaim　c) make fun of　d) encourage

2. query:　　a) suspicion　b) surprise　c) superstition　d) question

3. arid:　　a) doubtful　b) threatening　c) snowy　d) dry

4. enlighten:　　a) light a candle　b) educate　c) make less heavy　d) spin

5. quest:　　a) chest cold　b) pulsating star　c) search　d) feat of climbing

B. Words in Context

Supply the proper form of the most appropriate vocabulary word.

assail	foster	jaunty	query	reliable	reservoir	zealous

1. During last year's dry spell, the city _____ was reduced to a very low level, and the mayor told people not to use water unnecessarily.

2. The manager of the hotel answered my letter by saying only, "Your _____ about a part-time job is being given due consideration."

3. The Chamber of Commerce does much to _____ community development.

4. One hardly notices how threadbare the old poet's clothing is because she wears it with such a(n) _____ air and lectures in such a lively manner.

5. Within a year after the territory was opened to settlement, the pioneers began to work (enthusiastically) _____ for schools.

6. Regular exercise, a balanced diet, and plenty of sleep _____ both physical and mental health.

7. The mayor _____ the town council, charging that the _____ they planned was not large enough to provide for the city's water needs.

8. When buying any electrical appliance, two things are most important: price and _____.

60　Lesson 53 ▪ FOSTER/RESERVOIR

lesson 54

-graph- ▪ -scrib-

-graph-	(root)		**-scrib-**	(root)
ORIGIN:	Greek *graphein* (to write)		ORIGIN:	Latin *scribere* (to write)
MEANING:	To write		MEANING:	To write
CONTEXT:	"auto*graph*"		CONTEXT:	"in*scribe*"
OTHER FORM:	-gram- (telegram)		OTHER FORM:	-script- (scriptures)

A. Focus on Meaning

In each of the italicized words below, underline the word part that you have learned. Then, using your knowledge of the meaning of the word part, circle the letter of the best meaning for the italicized word.

1. *autobiography* of Johnson: a) picture   b) special car   c) life story written by the subject
   d) length of time in the White House

2. *transcribe* the notes: a) read   b) change   c) copy   d) destroy

3. the lawyer's *stenographer*:   a) one who advises   b) one who writes shorthand
   c) one who testifies in court   d) one who supplies bail

4. *capacity* of the tank: a) that which it holds   b) color   c) cost   d) metal weight

5. *scribbled* on the desk: a) propped   b) painted   c) wrote   d) spilled

6. Sandburg's *biography* of Lincoln: a) speech   b) statue   c) anecdote   d) life story

7. *admit* the group: a) turn away   b) speak to   c) send in   d) ignore

8. an *epigram* by Wilde: a) watercolor picture   b) elaborate musical composition
   c) witty, short piece of writing   d) lecture to scholars

B. REVIEW

Match the correct definition to each vocabulary word. Write the letter for the definition on the line.

_____ 1. arid   a. search

_____ 2. assail   b. lively

_____ 3. picket   c. dry

_____ 4. chasm   d. inform

_____ 5. quest   e. attack

_____ 6. spite   f. ill will

_____ 7. enlighten   g. abyss

_____ 8. jaunty   h. demonstrate against

lesson 55

obstinate ▪ clamber

obstinate   (adj)   (ˈob-stə-nət)

ORIGIN: Latin *obstare* (oppose)

MEANING: Holding to a purpose, course, or opinion in spite of reason persuasion, or evidence

CONTEXT: "Tim's *obstinate* behavior causes many problems because he insists on doing things his way rather than listening to the suggestions of others."

SYNONYMS: stubborn, dogged, mulish, unyielding

ANTONYMS: yielding, flexible, pliant, pliable

OTHER FORMS: obstinacy (n.), obstinateness (n.), obstinately (adv.)

clamber   (v)   (ˈklam-[b]ər)

ORIGIN: Middle English *clambren* (to climb)

MEANING: Climb with effort, with difficulty, or awkwardly

CONTEXT: "The young child *clambered* up the embankment and finally reached the level yard."

SYNONYM: scramble

NOTE: Do not confuse with clamor, which means a loud uproar.

A. Focus on Meaning

Circle the letter of the best meaning for each vocabulary word.

1. obstinate: a) sure   b) stubborn   c) sturdy   d) flexible

2. clamber: a) shout   b) clobber   c) scramble   d) clash

3. foster: a) encourage   b) hinder   c) start   d) plan

4. obstinate: a) unyielding   b) submissive   c) constructive   d) clumsy

5. clamber: a) call   b) climb with difficulty   c) climb easily   d) slide

B. Words in Context

Supply the proper form of the most appropriate vocabulary word.

arid   clamber   enlighten   obstinate

1. The central part of the state of Washington is so _____ that a native of the Sahara might feel at home.

2. The lecture on the energy shortage _____ many who had failed to realize the urgency of the problem.

3. Those puppies _____ up the back steps remind me of my little sister when she was a baby.

4. If you use the shortcut, you will have to _____ over boulders and fallen trees.

5. Jon snatched the teddy bear from his brother and _____ refused to give it back even though he had several of his own.

Shades of Meaning

- obstinate
- stubborn
- dogged
- mulish
- unyielding

Obstinate implies a stubborn or unreasonable persistence. *Stubborn* implies toughness in resisting attempts to change or let go of a course or opinion. *Dogged* suggests holding fast frequently with a sullen relentlessness. *Mulish* implies a completely unreasonable stubbornness. *Unyielding* suggests a lack of softness or willingness to change.

lesson 56

oration ▪ ardent

oration	(n)	(ə-´rā-shən)		**ardent**	(adj)	(´árd-nt)
ORIGIN:	Latin *orare* (to plead, to speak)			ORIGIN:	Latin *ardere* (to burn)	
MEANING:	A formal speech, especially one given on a special occasion			MEANING:	Having warm, intense feeling, emotion, or devotion	
CONTEXT:	"The *oration* Juanita gave in the speech contest won first place. "			CONTEXT:	"Being an *ardent* patriot, Mrs. Hess flies the flag in front of her home every day."	
SYNONYMS:	speech, declamation, discourse, address			SYNONYMS:	fervid, eager, enthusiastic, vehement, impassioned, warm	
OTHER FORMS:	orator (n.), oratory (n.), oratorical (adj.)			ANTONYMS:	apathetic, cool	
				OTHER FORMS:	ardently (adv.), ardor (n.)	

A. Focus on Meaning

Circle the letter of the word in each group that does not belong.

1. a) oration   b)speech   c) ornament   d) declamation

2. a)ardent   b) eager   c) fervid   d) cool

3. a) submissive   b) stubborn   c) obstinate   d) mulish

4. a) clamber   b) scramble   c) climb   d) cry

5. a) oratory   b) ardor   c) talk   d) speaking

6. a) ardent   b) apathetic   c) vehement   d) impassioned

B. Words in Context

Supply the proper form of the most appropriate vocabulary word.

anecdote	ardent	exploits	foster	obstinate	orator	query	reservoir

1. Susan B. Anthony was a(n) _____ advocate of voting rights for women.

2. Patrick Henry is remembered as the great _____ who said, "Give me liberty or give me death."

3. Father said, "Evelyn, you are as _____ as the old mule my grandfather used to have on his farm."

4. The lake is a natural _____ of water for irrigating the arid land many miles to the south.

5. High taxes do not _____ growth of savings and business investments.

6. The entire class in public speaking will take part in the _____ contest.

7. Veronica was fascinating to be around. She could tell many _____ about her _____ as a paratrooper.

8. Reference librarians must handle many different kinds of _____ every day.

9. Angela is an _____ gardener; she cannot resist flower shows or gardening centers.

lesson 57

comply ▪ utensil

comply (v) (kəm-ˈplī)

ORIGIN: Latin *complere* (to complete)

MEANING: To conform or adapt one's actions to a rule, to what is necessary, or to another's wishes

CONTEXT: "You must *comply* with the rules of the game or quit playing.

SYNONYMS: follow, yield to, assent to, obey

ANTONYMS: disregard, resist, disobey

OTHER FORMS: compliance (n.), compliant (adj.), compliancy (n.)

utensil (n) (yu̇-ˈten[t]-səl)

ORIGIN: Latin *utensilis* (useful)

MEANING: A useful vessel, tool, or implement

CONTEXT: "When you are ready to bake the cake, you will find baking *utensils* on the lower shelf of the cabinet."

SYNONYMS: implement, tool, container

A. Focus on Meaning

Match each word with its synonym by writing the proper letter in the blank.

1. comply_____   2. utensil _____   3. oration _____

4. ardent _____   5. compliant _____   6. obstinate_____

a) speech   b) conform   c) stubborn   d) yielding   e) tool   f) enthusiastic

B. Words in Context

Supply the proper form of the most appropriate vocabulary word.

assail	clamber	comply	obstinate	utensil	vibrate

1. When filling in the order form, _____ with the instructions for marking size, color, and style, or you may get something you do not want.

2. My _____ little sister refused to come to dinner when she was called.

3. The frying pan and coffee pot were the old prospector's only cooking _____.

4. In _____ with Mother's wishes, I will come home from the rock concert by midnight.

5. _____ over the fence, Laurie caught her jeans on the wire and tore them.

6. Burros are _____ little animals, moving only when and as fast as they desire; no amount of prodding will spur them.

7. The telephone wire (shook) _____ when the birds landed on it.

8. The candidate for the school board hurt his chances for election when he _____ his opponent with charges of corruption.

C. Antonyms

Circle the letter of the word whose meaning is most nearly opposite the vocabulary word.

1. zealous   a) passionate   b) eager   c) lazy   d) indifferent

2. ardent   a) apathetic   b) burning   c) vehement   d) lively

3. reliable   a) trustworthy   b) liable   c) envious   d) irresponsible

4. obstinate   a) stubborn   b) flexible   c) dry   d) mulish

5. arid   a) dry   b) parched   c) moist   d) hard

6. foster   a) store   b) nourish   c) discourage   d) disobey

lesson 58

mis- ▪ contra-

mis-	(prefix)
ORIGIN:	Anglo Saxon *mis* (wrong) or Latin *minus* (less)
MEANING:	Wrong, bad, poor, not
CONTEXT:	"*mis*print"

contra-	(prefix)
ORIGIN:	Latin *contra* (against)
MEANING:	Against, opposite
CONTEXT:	"*contra*diction"
OTHER FORM:	counter- (counterfeit)

A. Focus on Meaning

In each of the italicized words below, underline the word part that you have learned. Then, using your knowledge of the meaning of the word part, circle the letter of the best meaning for the italicized word.

1. serious *mischance*:   a) intention   b) illness   c) bad luck   d) result

2. *contraband* goods: a) transported against the law   b) permitted
   c) badly needed for manufacturing clothing   d) imported

3. to *contravene* the law: a) to obey   b) go against
   c) to interpret   d) to blame for one's troubles

4. *abducted* the small girl: a) protected   b) fed
   c) led away; kidnapped   d) showed the way; taught

5. *telegraph* the company: a) get in touch with   b) signal
   c) send a written message   d) pay

6. moves *counterclockwise*:   a) as the clock hands move   b) opposite to the clock hands
   c) faster than the clock hands   d) at the speed of the clock hands

B. REVIEW

Match the correct definition to each vocabulary word. Write the letter for the definition on the line.

_____ 1. oration   a. flaw

_____ 2. defect   b. scramble

_____ 3. obstinate   c. impassioned

_____ 4. exploit   d. abuse

_____ 5. afflict   e. speech

_____ 6. clamber   f. torment

_____ 7. valor   g. bravery

_____ 8. ardent   h. stubborn

lesson 59

controversy ▪ rave

controversy (n) (ˈkän-trə-ˌvər-sē)

ORIGIN: Latin *contra* (against) + *versus* (to turn)

MEANING: A dispute involving the expression of opposing views

CONTEXT: "In the board meeting there was quite a *controversy* over raising salaries, and several members became angry and walked out."

SYNONYMS: disagreement, argument, wrangle, debate, contention, quarrel:

ANTONYMS: agreement, accord

OTHER FORMS: controversial (adj.), controversially (adv.), controvert (v.)

rave (v) (rāv)

ORIGIN: Middle English *raven* (to wander, be delirious)

MEANING: To speak or write with extreme enthusiasm or as if in a frenzy

CONTEXT: "Mrs. Danner *raved* about her daughter's musical ability until the other mothers decided to ignore her."

SYNONYMS: praise, rant, bluster

A. Focus on Meaning

Circle the letter of the best meaning for each vocabulary word.

1. controversy: a) boxing match   b) cooperation   c) enemy   d) disagreement

2. rave: a) argue   b) confer   c) blister   d) praise

3. comply: a) assent   b) resist   c) send away   d) entertain

4. controversial: a) disputable   b) enterprising   c) successful   d) knowledgeable

5. zealous: a) useful   b) thermal   c) influential   d) eager

B. Words in Context

Supply the proper form of the most appropriate vocabulary word.

ardent	controversy	enlighten	oration	quest	rave

1. It was amusing to hear the critics _____ over those odd-looking pictures on display at the art museum.

2. My brother, who considers himself an authority on practically everything, delivered his weekly _____ on the superiority of ballet to modern dance.

3. While the _____ over raising the salaries of bus drivers continues, school remains closed.

4. Mother says she is inclined to agree with the bus drivers, although she usually _____ supports the position of the school board.

5. At the end of a thirty-hour bargaining session, union and company officials reached a compromise in the bitter _____ over wage increases.

6. For two days Enrique would not stop _____ about passing the chemistry test with a perfect score.

7. Ashley went from shop to shop on her _____ to find the perfect blouse for the party.

8. The lecture before the concert _____ us about the composer and the music we were about to hear.

lesson 60
prevail ▪ bounteous

prevail (v) (pri-´vā[ə]l)

ORIGIN:	Latin *prae* (before) + *valere* (to be strong)
MEANING:	To urge successfully
CONTEXT:	"Sue *prevailed* on me to go to the film even though I knew I should study."
MEANING:	To be widespread; to exist as an important feature
CONTEXT:	"Dead silence prevailed following the announcement."
SYNONYMS:	overcome, predominate, induce, triumph, succeed, persuade, persist, pervade
OTHER FORMS:	prevalence (n.), prevalent (adj.), prevalently (adv.)

bounteous (adj) (´baǔnt-ē-əs)

ORIGIN:	Latin *bonus* (good)
MEANING:	Freely given, generous, plentiful, abundant, ample
CONTEXT:	"The community responded to the needs of the destitute family with *bounteous* food and clothing."
SYNONYMS:	abundant, bountiful, profuse, copious, generous
ANTONYMS:	stingy, inadequate, meager
OTHER FORMS:	bounty (n.), bounteously (adv.), bounteousness (n.)

A. Focus on Meaning

Circle the letter of the word in each group that does not belong.

1. a) prevail   b) overcome   c) triumph   d) preview

2. a) bounteous   b) abundant   c) meager   d) profuse

3. a) controversy   b) disagreement   c) contention   d) agreement

4. a) prevalence   b) failure   c) persistence   d) predominance

5. a) bounty   b) abundance   c) lack   d) generosity

6. a) rave   b) rant   c) bluster   d) blame

B. Words in Context

Supply the proper form of the most appropriate vocabulary word.

bounteous	comply	foster	jaunty	prevail	utensil

1. The _____ reward Sandra received for finding Mr. Stone's billfold was enough to finish paying for her clarinet.

2. Westerly winds _____ over the greater part of the United States.

3. In filling out the application, _____ with the instructions.

4. Fall is a time when hurricanes are most _____ off the southeastern coast of the United States.

5. Thanksgiving is a time for celebrating the _____ of the harvest.

6. If you can carry only one _____ on the camping trip, Alicia, you should take your small Scout mess kit, because it is designed to serve several different functions.

7. Vanessa spoke up boldly at the assembly, urging everyone to _____ the Thanksgiving food drive this year.

8. When Mary Beth's name was called for the science award, she skipped _____ up the steps to the stage.

review/test

LESSONS 41–60

For each numbered word choose the word or phrase that is closest to the meaning of the
vocabulary word. Write the letter for the word on the line provided.

1. covet   a) supply   b) envy   1. _____

               c) teem   d) project

2. quest   a) question   b) query   2. _____

               c) search   d) abuse

3. render   a) provide   b) assign   3. _____

               c) malign   d) desire

4. exploit   a) explain   b) flex   4. _____

               c) express   d) abuse

5. controversy a) accord   b) agreement   5. _____

               c) fear   d) quarrel

6. awe   a) hunt   b) reverence   6. _____

               c) praise   d) enthusiasm

7. cope   a) pursue   b) resist   7. _____

               c) live with   d) enter

8. anecdote   a) remedy   b) cure   8. _____

               c) tale   d) relief

9. arid   a) moist   b) parched   9. _____

               c) wet   d) mistreated

10. prevail   a) prevent   b) succeed   10. _____

               c) agree   d) obey

11. foster   a) neglect   b) discourage   11. _____

               c) nuture   d) desire

12. ardent   a) enthusiastic b) cool   12. _____

               c) apathetic   d) feared

13. obstinate   a) flexible   b) pliant   13. _____
c) scrambled   d) stubborn

14. ascribe   a) envy   b) attribute   14. _____
c) deny   d) deliver

15. jaunty   a) dull   b) slow   15. _____
c) lively   d) wild

16. penetrate   a) crave   b) supply   16. _____
c) assault   d) pierce

17. comply   a) obey   b) disobey   17. _____
c) resist   d) furnish

18. attire   a) sketch   b) clothes   18. _____
c) blouse   d) mission

19. zealous   a) indifferent   b) apathetic   19. _____
c) passionate   d) truthful

20. oration   a) prayer   b) silence   20. _____
c) expression   d) speech

Test Tips

Some vocabulary tests are antonym tests. As you already know from the lessons in this book, antonyms are words that mean the opposite on one another. Antonym tests, as you have already seen in the "Antonym" exercises in this book, may try to trick you by including a synonym or two as possible answers. Remember that the test asks for the word that means the opposite of the vocabulary word.

Practice: On the line provided write the letter for the word that means the opposite of the numbered word .

1. reliable   (a) irresponsible   (b) dependable   1 _____
(c) trustworthy   (d) disturbed

2. bounteous   (a) abundant   (b) beautiful   2. _____
(c) stingy   (d) reserved

3. comply   (a) obey   (b) complain   3. _____
(c) follow   (d) resist

4. obstinate   (a) stubborn   (b) friendly   4. _____
(c) flexible   (d) clever

lesson 61

advocate ▪ curtail

advocate	(v)	('ad-və-kāt)
ORIGIN:	Latin *ad* (toward) + *vocare* (to call)	
MEANING:	To speak in favor of and support publicly	
CONTEXT:	"The mayor *advocates* higher salaries for all city employees."	
SYNONYMS:	recommend, support, urge, favor	
ANTONYMS:	disapprove, oppose	
OTHER FORM:	advocate (n. meaning "person who speaks in favor of")	

curtail	(v)	(kər-'tā[ə]l)
ORIGIN:	Latin *curtus* (short)	
MEANING:	To cut short, to reduce	
CONTEXT:	"Because of illness, Father is forced to *curtail* his activities."	
SYNONYMS:	lessen, shorten, diminish	
ANTONYMS:	increase, enlarge	
OTHER FORM:	curtailment (n.)	

A. Focus on Meaning

Circle the letter of the best meaning for each vocabulary word.

1. advocate: a) call   b) oppose   c) recommend   d) diminish

2. curtail: a) enlarge   b) lessen   c) cover   d) surround

3. prevail: a) persuade   b) prevent   c) fail   d) cover

4. advocate: a) supporter   b) judge   c) reporter   d) opponent

5. curtail: a) correct   b) lengthen   c) multiply   d) diminish

B. Words in Context

Supply the proper form of the most appropriate vocabulary word.

advocate	clamber	controversy	curtail	rave	reservoir

1. Eve Williams thinks the government should take a more active role in helping the poor, and she _____ increased government spending for welfare programs.

2. Liz grew tired of hearing Meg _____ about all her new clothes.

3. The president suggested that there would be a(n) _____ in the expenditure of federal funds for highways if Congress enacted budget cutbacks.

4. The _____ over whether Interstate 40 should be constructed through Overton Park in Memphis was long and unpleasant.

5. It is hoped that something will be done to _____ the rising cost of living.

6. Pete Seeger, a well-known folk singer, was a leading _____ of preventing industries from polluting our country's waterways.

7. Our hiking party _____ up the trail on Bear Mountain, reaching the shelter before the storm hit.

8. Because it was leaking badly, the engineer urged that funds be put aside to repair the town water _____ very soon.

celestial ▪ grope

celestial	(adj)	(sə-ˈles[h]-chəl)

ORIGIN: Latin *caelum* (heaven)

MEANING: Of or pertaining to the sky or the heavens

CONTEXT: "Stars are *celestial* bodies."

SYNONYMS: heavenly, divine, unearthly, solar, astral

OTHER FORM: celestially (adv.)

grope	(v)	(grōp)

ORIGIN: Old English *grap* (a grasp)

MEANING: To feel one's way; to search blindly

CONTEXT: "I had to *grope* in the darkness until I found the flashlight."

SYNONYMS: fumble, feel, hunt, search

A. Focus on Meaning

Circle the letter of the word in each group that does not belong.

1. a) earthly   b) heavenly   c) astral   d) solar

2. a) grope   b) feel   c) fumble   d) seize

3. a) advocate   b) recommend   c) oppose   d) support

4. a) gripe   b) hunt   c) search   d) fumble

5. a) celestial   b) divine   c) hellish   d) unearthly

6. a) curtail   b) lessen   c) shorten   d) enlarge

B. Words in Context

Supply the proper form of the most appropriate vocabulary word.

arid	bounteous	celestial	comply	grope	prevail

1. _____ navigation involves observing the position of heavenly bodies.

2. After _____ in the darkness and stumbling over several pieces of furniture, Mary Anne finally found the light switch.

3. "Dad," said Manuel, "can I _____ on you to let me use the car tonight?"

4. There is a(n) _____ supply of nuts and acorns for the squirrels this winter.

5. The principal told Harry that if he would not _____ with the regulation governing physical examinations, he could not return to school.

6. Nearly one-third of the entire continent of Africa is one vast, _____ wasteland known as the Sahara.

7. Do you think that _____ travel to planets outside of our solar system will ever be possible?

8. Last night Doug dropped his car keys in the dark parking lot and _____ about for them for ten minutes before he finally found them.

lesson 63

in- ▪ dis-

in-	(prefix)		**dis-**	(prefix)
ORIGIN:	Latin *in* (not, into)		ORIGIN:	Latin *dis* (apart)
MEANING:	Not		MEANING:	Not
CONTEXT:	"*in*correct"		CONTEXT:	"*dis*honest"
MEANING:	In, into, within		MEANING:	Apart from, away
CONTEXT:	"*in*hale"		CONTEXT:	"*dis*connect"
OTHER FORMS:	im- (impale), ig- (ignoble), ir- (irrelevant), il- (illegible)		OTHER FORMS:	di- (digress), dif- (diffuse)

A. Focus on Meaning

In each of the italicized words below, underline the word parts that you have learned. Then, using your knowledge of the meanings of the word parts, circle the letter of the best meaning for the italicized word. (For some words there may be only one word part.)

1. *invalid* testimony: a) valuable b) not true c) from a sick person d) boring

2. *divert* the water: a) cross b) purify c) turn away d) turn off

3. *misgivings* about the trip: a) feelings of doubt b) slides c) hopes d) books

4. *immigrate* to the United States: a) come into b) leave c) become a citizen d) support

5. *digress* from the subject: a) learn b) stray c) be inspired d) be bored

6. *displease* the boss: a) fire b) help c) inspire d) offend

7. to *inject* comedy: a) take out b) put in c) increase d) prescribe

8. *dislodged* the rocks: a) crushed b) removed c) replaced d) secured

9. use of a *countermeasure*: a) an opposing plan b) a supporting plan
   c) a better plan d) an old plan

B. REVIEW

Match the correct definition to each vocabulary word. Write the letter of the definition on the line.

_____ 1. controversy   a. overcome

_____ 2. magnitude   b. abundant

_____ 3. prevail   c. diminish

_____ 4. advocate   d. control

_____ 5. dominate   e. praise

_____ 6. rave   f. hugeness

_____ 7. bounteous   g. argument

_____ 8. curtail   h. support

lesson 64
maze ▪ indifferent

maze (n) (māz)

ORIGIN: Middle English *masen* (puzzle)

MEANING: A confusing, intricate network of passages; a state of confusion

CONTEXT: "In applying for the position, she had to work her way through a *maze* of paperwork and interviews."

SYNONYMS: muddle, complex, labyrinth

indifferent (adj) (in-´dif-ərnt)

ORIGIN: Latin *in* (not) + *differe* (to bear apart, put off)

MEANING: Showing neither like nor dislike, neither concern nor unconcern

CONTEXT: "She was *indifferent* to the troubles of others, perhaps because she was always so concerned about herself."

SYNONYMS: unconcerned, neutral disinterested, detached, apathetic

ANTONYMS: concerned, committed

OTHER FORM: indifference (n.), indifferently (adv.)

A. Focus on Meaning

Match each word with its synonym by writing the proper letter in the blank.

1. maze _____
2. indifference _____
3. celestial _____
4. grope _____
5. cope _____
6. indifferent _____

a) heavenly   b) feel   c) apathy   d) unconcerned   e) combat   f) labyrinth

B. Words in Context

Supply the proper form of the most appropriate vocabulary word.

advocate	chasm	curtail	indifferent	maze	obstinate	version

1. Her application was lost in a(n) _____ of bureaucratic red tape.

2. The doctor told Jerry to _____ his reading until his glasses were ready.

3. The boy's _____ to food was a puzzle to the gourmet cook.

4. Rats will learn to find their way through a complex _____ to get food.

5. I know Carla must be ill; she is so _____ to the plans for the dance.

6. The president is a(n) _____ of arms limitations.

7. Mother's (account) _____ of the disagreement is that neither the school board nor the bus drivers will accept a compromise.

8. The senator _____ refused to change his decision even though he suspected that millions of dollars would be wasted on the unnecessary project.

9. Canyonlands National Park in southern Utah is awesome, a vast _____ of rocks and _____.

10. In every basketball game, Ivy is very intent; she is totally _____ to everything else going on around her.

lesson 65

discredit ▪ adjacent

discredit   (v)   (dis-ˈkred-ət)

ORIGIN: Latin *dis* (not) + *credere* (to believe, to trust)

MEANING: To refuse to accept as true or accurate or to cause disbelief in

CONTEXT: "Because he has lied to me in the past, I *discredit* what he is saying now."

SYNONYMS: disbelieve, doubt, mistrust

ANTONYMS: believe, credit, trust

adjacent   (adj)   (ə-ˈjās-nt)

ORIGIN: Latin *adjacere* (to be near)

MEANING: Lying next to, nearby

CONTEXT: "Because the vacant lot *adjacent* to ours belongs to a friend who lives out of town, I keep it mowed, and she allows our children to play on it."

SYNONYMS: bordering, adjoining, abutting, contiguous

ANTONYM: distant

OTHER FORMS: adjacently (adv.), adjacency (n.)

A. Focus on Meaning

Circle the letter of the best meaning for each vocabulary word.

1. discredit: a) repay   b) endorse   c) bribe   d) doubt

2. adjacent: a) bordering   b) floral   c) vacant   d) cheerful

3. maze: a) nest   b) pagan religion   c) knob   d) muddle

4. indifferent: a) same   b) unconcerned   c) lazy   d) weak

5. rave: a) float   b) bluster   c) agree   d) drown

B. Words in Context

Supply the proper form of the most appropriate vocabulary word.

adjacent	celestial	discredit

1. I hope the teacher assigns me the seat _____ to Carlos.

2. It is possible to determine a direction at night if you are familiar with the positions of some of the _____ bodies.

3. The president made several attempts to _____ the ideas of his opponents by calling them "big spenders."

4. The cafeteria is _____ to the dormitory so that students don't have too far to walk in bad weather.

5. James, my younger brother, has told so many tall tales that it is hard not to _____ everything he says.

Shades of Meaning
- adjacent
- adjoining
- bordering
- abutting
- contiguous

Adjacent may or may not imply contact but always implies that nothing is in between. *Adjoining* definitely implies meeting and touching at some point or line. *Bordering* suggests touching at the edge or boundary. *Abutting* suggests having contact with something else at a boundary or dividing line. *Contiguous* implies having contact on all or most of one side.

lesson 66

divert ▪ aloof

divert	(v)	(də-ˈvərt)
ORIGIN:	Latin *divertere* (to turn in different directions)	
MEANING:	To turn from one use or course to another	
CONTEXT:	"She *diverted* the little boy from throwing rocks to putting them into his pail."	
SYNONYMS:	deflect, distract, beguile, turn aside	
OTHER FORMS:	diversion (n.)	

aloof	(adj)	(ə-ˈlüf)
ORIGIN:	Obsolete English *aloof* (to windward)	
MEANING:	Distant, especially in feelings or interest	
CONTEXT:	"Mother adopted an *aloof* attitude toward the brothers' argument, taking neither side."	
SYNONYMS:	distant, impartial, uninvolved, remote	
ANTONYMS:	close, involved, committed	
OTHER FORMS:	aloof (adv.), aloofness (n.)	

A. Focus on Meaning

Circle the letter of the best meaning for each vocabulary word.

1. divert: a) encourage   b) turn aside   c) split in two   d) harass

2. aloof: a) distant   b) intense   c) complicated   d) interested

3. discredit: a) believe   b) sell   c) misbehave   d) mistrust

4. adjacent: a) remote   b) above   c) related to mathematics   d) nearby

5. aloof: a) uninvolved   b) close   c) foolish   d) kind

6. divert: a) merge   b) play   c) deflect   d) concentrate

B. Words in Context

Supply the proper form of the most appropriate vocabulary word.

aloof   comply   divert   maze

1. Television can be a worthwhile _____ from work or study if one selects programs wisely.

2. Dad shouted as Bob backed out of the garage, "Either _____ with my wishes and have the car back here for me at eight o'clock, or forget about using it tomorrow night."

3. The _____ author neither worried nor cared about public opinion.

4. Mother says that I need to learn to concentrate, that I am too easily _____ from studying.

5. The _____ of concrete walks detracts from the beauty of the place, but it prevents the grass from being trampled by runners who sprint across the park.

C. Antonyms

Circle the letter of the word whose meaning is most nearly opposite the vocabulary word.

1. comply   a) disobey   b) obey   c) follow   d) search

2. advocate   a) favor   b) recommend   c) advance   d) oppose

3. indifferent   a) concerned   b) neutral   c) detached   d) strange

4. controversy   a) debate   b) quarrel   c) agreement   d) turning point

5. bounteous   a) generous   b) stingy   c) abundant   d) beautiful

6. curtail   a) diminish   b) favor   c) increase   d) endure

lesson 67

-pon- ▪ multi-

-pon-	(root)		multi-	(prefix)
ORIGIN:	Latin *ponere* (to place)		ORIGIN:	Latin *multus* (many)
MEANING:	To place or put		MEANING:	More than one, many
CONTEXT:	"post*pone*"		CONTEXT:	"*multi*plication"
OTHER FORMS:	-pose- (impose), -posit- (deposit)			

A. Focus on Meaning

In each of the italicized words below, underline the word part that you have learned. Then, using your knowledge of the meaning of the word part, circle the letter of the best meaning for the italicized word.

1. a *multicellular* organism: a) having many cells   b) having few cells
   c) composed mainly of stones   d) lacking cells

2. a sincere *exponent* of the faith: a) person supporting a position   b) doubter
   c) person who serves as an interpreter   d) believer

3. *multifarious* activities: a) strange and intense   b) humorous
   c) undesirable   d) varied and numerous

4. disapprove of her *misbehavior*:   a) benevolence   b) acting wrong
   c) jauntiness   d) aloofness

5. *position* of power: a) place   b) sense
   c) rejection   d) effect

6. a *multipurpose* instrument: a) obsolete   b) having many uses
   c) musical   d) legal

B. REVIEW

Match the correct definition to each vocabulary word. Write the letter of the definition on the line.

_____ 1. indifferent   a. overcome

_____ 2. prevail   b. nearby

_____ 3. discredit   c. disinterested

_____ 4. controversy   d. abundant

_____ 5. maze   e. labyrinth

_____ 6. bounteous   f. shorten

_____ 7. adjacent   g. disbelieve

_____ 8. curtail   h. disagreement

conspire ▪ disperse

conspire	(v)	(kən-ˈspī[ə]r)
ORIGIN:	Latin *conspirare* (unite)	
MEANING:	To agree to work and act together, especially secretly in order to do something wrong	
CONTEXT:	"They *conspired* to kill the queen, but their plan was discovered by Scotland Yard before they could carry it out."	
SYNONYMS:	plot, contrive, scheme	
OTHER FORMS:	conspiracy (n.), conspirator (n.), conspirative (adj.)	

disperse	(v)	(dis-ˈpərs)
ORIGIN:	Latin *dispergere* (to scatter)	
MEANING:	To drive, to spread, to send, to scatter in various directions	
CONTEXT:	"The police *dispersed* the crowd, telling them to go to their homes."	
SYNONYMS:	scatter, disband	
ANTONYMS:	combine, collect	
OTHER FORMS:	dispersion (n.), dispersive (adj.)	

A. Focus on Meaning

Match each word with its synonym by writing the proper letter in the blank.

1. conspire _____
2. disperse _____
3. divert _____
4. conspirator _____
5. dispersion _____
6. aloof _____

a) deflect   b) one who plots   c) scattering   d) distant   e) plot   f) scatter

B. Words in Context

Supply the proper form of the most appropriate vocabulary word.

adjacent	conspire	curtail	discredit	disperse	grope

1. Amy and her two little sisters joined forces in a(n) _____ to empty the cookie jar without their mother's knowledge.

2. After a few minutes the two giant exhaust fans almost _____ the cloud of sulfur dioxide that had swept through the laboratory during the experiment.

3. My great uncle and my grandfather bought _____ houses so that the family could stay together.

4. The gang _____ to slip into the room during the lunch period and take a copy of the test.

5. The defense attorney sought to _____ the testimony of the witness by leading her to admit that she was not wearing her eyeglasses when she identified the defendant.

6. It is amazing how quickly the crowd _____ from the new stadium.

7. Puzzled by the team's poor play, the coach spent the day _____ for answers.

8. Tanya _____ her dance practice because her knee began to bother her.

vitality ▪ suppress

vitality (n) (vī-ˈtal-ət-ē)

ORIGIN: Latin *vita* (life)

MEANING: Great physical or mental vigor; capacity for enduring

CONTEXT: "Only prisoners with great *vitality* were able to survive the camps. "

SYNONYMS: vigor, strength, robustness

ANTONYM: weakness

OTHER FORMS: vital (adj.), vitalization (n.)

suppress (v) (sə-ˈpres)

ORIGIN: Latin *supprimere* (to press under)

MEANING: To put down or to keep from public knowledge by authority or force

CONTEXT: "An effort was made to *suppress* information about the scandal by closing the trial to reporters."

SYNONYMS: subdue, hold down, repress

ANTONYMS: release, distribute, broadcast

OTHER FORMS: suppression (n.), suppressive (adj.)

A. Focus on Meaning

Circle the letter of the best meaning for each vocabulary word.

1. bestow: a) criticize b) give c) kneel d) bow

2. suppress: a) subdue b) poison c) strengthen d) submit

3. conspire: a) hesitate b) scheme c) sketch d) enhance

4. disperse: a) return b) wait c) scatter d) operate

5. vitality: a) antenna b) strength c) vitamin d) knowledge

B. Words in Context

Supply the proper form of the most appropriate vocabulary word.

| advocate | bounteous | conspire | divert | suppress | vitality |

1. Was there a(n) _____ to kill Martin Luther King, Jr., or did the assassin work alone?

2. Cal Ripkin, Jr. was an athlete of such extraordinary health and _____ that he played professional baseball for years without missing a game.

3. In countries with totalitarian governments, the _____ of news is routine.

4. The rescue mission _____ the public's attention from other items in the news.

5. The seventy-year-old star, who danced for two hours every night in a musical comedy on Broadway, showed great _____.

6. It took all of Jody's self-control to _____ a giggle when the principal dropped the diplomas during the graduation ceremony.

7. "The weather has been perfect for strawberries, " said Mr. Horowitz. "We have never had such a _____ harvest.

8. Kirk is a strong _____ for clean air and clean water.

insomnia ▪ whet

insomnia	(n)	(in-´sam-nē-ə)	**whet**	(v)	(hwet)

ORIGIN:	Latin *insomnis* (sleepless)	ORIGIN:	Old English *hwettan* (to make keen)
MEANING:	Prolonged inability to obtain sufficient sleep	MEANING:	To sharpen, to make keen, to stimulate
CONTEXT:	"Could his *insomnia* be caused by a guilty conscience?"	CONTEXT:	"The tales Aunt June told of the old house and its occupants *whetted* my curiosity."
SYNONYMS:	sleeplessness, wakefulness	SYNONYMS:	stimulate, arouse, sharpen, quicken, inspire
OTHER FORMS:	insomniac (n. meaning "a person who can't sleep")	ANTONYM:	dull, satisfy

A. Focus on Meaning

Circle the letter of the best meaning for each vocabulary word.

1. insomnia: a) slumber   b) sleeplessness   c) illness   d) something

2. whet: a) dampen   b) dull   c) arouse   d) arrive

3. vitality: a) vitamins   b) weakness   c) vibration   d) vigor

4. suppress: a) put down   b) smooth   c) release   d) express

5. insomnia: a) insolence   b) wakefulness   c) failure   d) sleepiness

6. whet: a) stimulate   b) satisfy   c) wet   d) wonder

B. Words in Context

Supply the proper form of the most appropriate vocabulary word.

aloof   insomnia   maze   suppress   vitality   whet

1. The delicious odors from the kitchen have _____ my appetite.

2. My grandmother, a(n) _____, spends half the night reading and watching TV.

3. The revolutionary troops who came through that grim winter at Valley Forge had great _____, or they never could have survived.

4. After six sleepless nights, Mrs. McLeod went to see her doctor, who prescribed sleeping tablets to relieve her _____.

5. Many children's desires to become sailors have been _____ by tales of the sea.

6. When I am with Betty, I try to _____ my hostile feelings toward Mary Evelyn, who is Betty's friend.

7. To Barbara, the corridors and hallways in the museum seemed like an endless _____.

8. Mr. Riley, our English teacher, remained _____ from the class elections.

lesson 71

-ten- ▪ -tend-

-ten-	(root)		**-tend-**	(root)
ORIGIN:	Latin *tenere* (to have or to hold)		ORIGIN:	Latin *tendere* (to stretch)
MEANING:	Hold, contain		MEANING:	To stretch
CONTEXT:	"*ten*acious"		CONTEXT:	"ex*tend*"
OTHER FORMS:	-tin- (continent), -tent- (content), -tain- (retain)		OTHER FORMS:	-tent- (extent), -tens- (tension)

A. Focus on Meaning

In each of the italicized words below, underline the word part that you have learned. Then, using your knowledge of the meaning of the word part, circle the letter of the best meaning for the italicized word.

1. her church's *tenet* on the matter: a) wish   b) opinion   c) belief held as true   d) indifference

2. a plant with *tendrils*:   a) flowers   b) berries   c) runners that hold   d) poison

3. *extenuate* a crime: a) commit   b) forgive   c) hold as less serious   d) punish.

4. *retain* the paper: a) burn   b) give away   c) hold onto   d) fold up

5. *ostentatious* generosity: a) spread out for show   b) secret   c) tremendous   d) unselfish

6. your *multiplicity* of errors: a) rejection   b) large number   c) acceptance   d) lack

7. *pertinent* details: a) holding to the subject   b) straying from the subject   c) graphic   d) many

B. REVIEW

Match the correct definition to each vocabulary word. Write the letter of the definition on the line.

_____ 1. conspire   a. scatter

_____ 2. discredit   b. distant

_____ 3. vitality   c. recommend

_____ 4. aloof   d. disbelieve

_____ 5. disperse   e. detached

_____ 6. advocate   f. hold down

_____ 7. suppress   g. vigor

_____ 8. indifferent   h. scheme

lesson 72

gait ▪ chafe

gait   (n)   (gāt)

ORIGIN: Middle English *gate* (way)

MEANING: Manner, style, or pattern of movement

CONTEXT: "The *gait* of the sick man as he walked down the street was slow and stumbling."

SYNONYMS: step, pace, walk, tread

chafe   (v)   (chāf)

ORIGIN: Latin *calefacere* (to make warm)

MEANING: To warm, wear away, or irritate by rubbing

CONTEXT: "Elsa's new shoes were so tight that they *chafed* her feet with every step."

SYNONYMS: rub, irritate, scrape

ANTONYMS: soothe, please

A. Focus on Meaning

Circle the letter of the word in each group that does not belong.

1.   a) gait   b) gate   c) pace   d) walk

2.   a) chafe   b) rub   c) irritate   d) chase

3.   a) insomnia   b) insolence   c) wakefulness   d) sleeplessness

4.   a) whet   b) gouge   c) stimulate   d) arouse

5.   a) gait   b) tread   c) step   d) hitch

6.   a) chafe   b) scrape   c) soothe   d) wear away

B. Words in Context

Supply the proper form of the most appropriate vocabulary word.

chafe   divert   gait   indifferent   suppress   vitality

1. An undernourished child has little _____.

2. My brother complained that the tight shirt collar _____ his neck.

3. Street demonstrations have often been _____ by arresting the leaders of protest movements.

4. Oxen move with a slow _____; horses are much faster.

5. Scuba diving can be a rewarding sport even though a diver must learn to tolerate the taste of bottled air and the _____ of heavy tanks against the skin.

6. Realizing that he was late, David spurred his horse to a faster _____, raising a trail of dust.

7. Josh, our German shepherd, is completely _____ to Darla's new puppy.

8. Stan shouted that we must do something quickly to _____ the water from the broken downspout away from the house.

lesson 73

etiquette ▪ harass

etiquette (n) (ˈet-i-kət)

ORIGIN: Old French *estiquer* (to stick)

MEANING: Conventional requirements controlling social behavior

CONTEXT: "The rules of *etiquette* say that when an elderly person enters a room, younger people should stand up as a sign of respect."

SYNONYMS: decorum, propriety, manners

harass (v) (hə-ˈras)

ORIGIN: Old French *harer* (to set a dog on)

MEANING: To attack, disturb, torment, bother repeatedly

CONTEXT: "Mother was so *harassed* by the children's questions, quarrels, wants, and needs that she could not get her work done."

SYNONYMS: badger, vex, fatigue, torment, trouble, pester

OTHER FORMS: harassment (n.), harassed (add.)

A. Focus on Meaning

Circle the letter of the best meaning for each vocabulary word.

1. etiquette: a) eating   b) manners   c) dessert   d) model

2. harass: a) ride   b) vex   c) promote   d) advance

3. gait: a) hedge   b) enclosure   c) voice   d) walk

4. chafe: a) irritate   b) enjoy   c) project   d) escape

5. etiquette: a) foreign exchange   b) virus   c) proper behavior   d) attraction

B. Words in Context

Supply the proper form of the most appropriate vocabulary word.

chafe	etiquette	disperse	gait	harass	insomnia	whet

1. Our picnic was pleasant except for the presence of mosquitoes that _____ us by continually buzzing around our heads.

2. "Mom, I'm not bothered by _____, just hunger," stated Mike when Mother found him in the kitchen after midnight.

3. Being told by the coach not to try even a single cigarette only _____ the desire of the foolish player.

4. Smooth the blanket under the saddle, or it will _____ your pony's back.

5. Margaret's broken leg has not healed completely, so she walks with a slow, careful _____ that is uncharacteristic of her.

6. It is not good _____ for you to sit while Aunt Eva is standing.

7. On the boardwalk at the beach we were _____ by brine flies until they were _____ by the brisk breezes.

8. Some research shows that getting four or five hours of sunlight or bright light during the day can help ease _____ for some people at night.

82   Lesson 73 • ETIQUETTE/HARASS

lesson 74

integrity ▪ grapple

integrity	(n)	(in-ˈteg-rət-ē)

ORIGIN: Latin *integer* (whole)

MEANING: Holding firmly to sound moral principles and standards

CONTEXT: "Mr. Davis has always been a man of *integrity*, and I am sure he will hold to the same high principles now that he has been elected to the legislature."

SYNONYMS: honesty, probity, honor

ANTONYMS: dishonesty, duplicity, baseness

grapple	(v)	(ˈgrap-əl)

ORIGIN: Old French *grape* (hook)

MEANING: To seize, to hold in a firm grip, or to engage in a struggle to hold firmly

CONTEXT: He was *grappling* with a man much larger than he and needed help to hold him until the police arrived."

SYNONYMS: struggle, wrestle, grasp, seize

A. Focus on Meaning

Circle the letter of the best meaning for each vocabulary word.

1. integrity: a) immorality b) grimace c) kindness d) uprightness
2. grapple: a) groan b) grumble c) grasp d) gasp
3. etiquette: a) integrity b) etching c) decorum d) calmness
4. grapple: a) struggle b) strain c) steer d) stomp
5. harass: a) help b) hurtle c) injure d) irritate

B. Words in Context

Supply the proper form of the most appropriate vocabulary word.

attire   conspire   gait   grapple   integrity   tassel

1. Alison, at thirteen months, has an unsteady _____ that will improve rapidly as she walks more.
2. The two men, _____ fiercely with one another, struggled to gain possession of the gun.
3. The prime minister and three of his lieutenants were _____ to rob the royal treasury until the palace guards uncovered their scheme.
4. The _____ on Patsy's cap is gold because she is in the Honor Society.
5. A coat is inadequate _____ for skiing, Jo Ellen.
6. Paul Tice should make a good business manager for the university because he is a person of great _____.

Shades of Meaning

- integrity
- honesty
- honor
- probity

Integrity implies trustworthiness and incorruptibility to such a degree that one is not capable of being false to a trust, responsibility, or pledge. *Honesty* implies refusal to lie, steal, or deceive in any way. *Honor* suggests an active regard and care for the standards of one's profession, calling, or position. *Probity* implies tried and proven honesty or integrity.

lesson 75

instigate ▪ wrath

instigate	(v)	(ˈin[t]-stə-ˌgāt)
ORIGIN:	Latin *instigare* (to stimulate)	
MEANING:	To start, to incite, to urge to some action or course	
CONTEXT:	"The school board *instigated* an investigation to determine whether funds had been misappropriated."	
SYNONYMS:	incite, encourage, start	
OTHER FORMS:	instigator (n.), instigation (n.)	

wrath	(n)	(rath)
ORIGIN:	Old English *wrath* (bad)	
MEANING:	Strong, fierce, or violent anger	
CONTEXT:	"The *wrath* of the citizens of the village when they heard of the attack upon the child knew no bounds."	
SYNONYMS:	rage fury, ire, anger	
OTHER FORMS:	wrathful (adj.), wrathfully (adv.)	

A. Focus on Meaning

Match each word with its synonym by writing the proper letter in the blank.

1. instigator _____   2. grapple _____   3. wrath _____

4. instigate _____   5. wrathful_____   6. integrity_____

a) initiator   b) fury   c) start   d) honor   e) angry   f) struggle

B. Words in Context

Supply the proper form of the most appropriate vocabulary word.

divert   etiquette   harass   instigate   integrity   whet   wrath

1. Look in any book on _____ for an explanation of your duties as an usher at your brother's wedding.

2. If you boys continue to harass the manager of the music shop, you can expect her _____ to descend on you.

3. Those crooks have no idea of the meaning of _____.

4. When Gene's big tom cat tired of being _____ by our dog Boots, he lunged toward her nose, causing her to move away and yelp with fear.

5. Spurred by many complaints from outraged citizens, the Justice Department _____ an inquiry into the nature and the scope of organized crime in the nation's capital.

6. Roy pounced _____ upon his little sister for having eaten his share of birthday cake.

7. The suspect tried to _____ the evidence from himself that he was the _____ of the rock throwing.

8. Previews try to _____ the audiences appetite for upcoming films.

lesson 76

-spec- ▪ com-

-spec-	(root)		**com-**	(prefix)
ORIGIN:	Latin *specere* (to look at)		ORIGIN:	Latin *cum* (with, together)
MEANING:	Look, see		MEANING:	With, together
CONTEXT:	"*spec*imen"		CONTEXT:	"*com*pany"
OTHER FORMS:	spit- (auspicious), -spect- (spectator)		OTHER FORMS:	con- (convocation), col- (collaborate), co- (cosponsor)

A. Focus on Meaning

In each of the italicized words below, underline the word parts that you have learned. Then, using your knowledge of the meanings of the word parts, circle the letter of the best meaning for the italicized word. (For some words there may be only one word part.)

1. lost her *spectacles*:   a) appetite   b) fishing tackle   c) wallet   d) eye glasses

2. an *incongruous* mixture of people: a) funny   b) lacking intelligence
   c) not belonging together   d) harmonious

3. *speculate* on the outcome: a) comment   b) gamble
   c) look at all possibilities   d) experiment with

4. *interpose* an obstacle: a) explain   b) remove   c) put in the way   d) refer to

5. *collateral* ridges of mountains: a) running at opposite ends of a range   b) very high
   c) very low   d) running together side by side

6. a *specious* argument: a) moral   b) heated   c) looking good only at first   d) loud

7. a *tense* moment: a) short   b) relaxed   c) strained   d) important

B. REVIEW

Match the correct definition to each vocabulary word. Write the letter of the definition on the line.

_____ 1. gait   a. torment

_____ 2. grapple   b. pace

_____ 3. chafe   c. vigor

_____ 4. divert   d. wrestle

_____ 5. integrity   e. manners

_____ 6. etiquette   f. deflect

_____ 7. vitality   g. honesty

_____ 8. harass   h. irritate

lesson 77

bigotry ▪ contemplate

bigotry	(n)	(ˊbig-ə-trē)	**contemplate**	(v)	(ˊkȧnt-əm-ˌplāt)

ORIGIN:	Middle French *bigot* (hypocrite)
MEANING:	Intolerance of any opinion, belief, or creed that is different from one's own
CONTEXT:	"The *bigotry* of the members of that sect is so great that they will not even listen to others' beliefs."
SYNONYMS:	dogmatism, intolerance
ANTONYMS:	tolerance, open-mindedness
OTHER FORMS:	bigot (n.)

ORIGIN:	Latin *contemplatus* (to observe)
MEANING:	To consider deeply and carefully for a long time
CONTEXT:	"After *contemplating* all the possible consequences of advancing the queen pawn, the chess champion chose to check his opponent's king with his bishop."
SYNONYMS:	meditate, ponder, study
OTHER FORMS:	contemplation (n.), contemplative (adj.)

A. Focus on Meaning

Circle the letter of the best meaning for each vocabulary word.

1. bigotry: a) intolerance   b) large object   c) buried treasure   d) fate
2. contemplate: a) pound   b) pull   c) ponder   d) paint
3. instigate: a) investigate   b) start   c) persuade   d) kidnap
4. grapple: a) trap   b) smirk   c) seize   d) turn
5. bigot: a) microphone   b) closed-minded person   c) faucet   d) insect

B. Words in Context

Supply the proper form of the most appropriate vocabulary word.

bigotry	contemplate	integrity	wrath

1. Mr. Morris is a(n) _____ who insists that all beliefs other than his own are false and should not be protected by the First Amendment.
2. Some people believe that the _____ of God was turned loose in this tempest.
3. We ought to question the _____ of a person who tries to take unfair advantage of another.
4. Mr. Wright's _____ is evident in his desire to prevent all ethnic minority members from being hired as college instructors.
5. After a moment or two of _____, Sam decided to skip lunch to study for the exam; he reasoned that getting a good grade was most important, and he knew he could eat a snack after school.

C. Antonyms

Circle the letter of the word whose meaning is most nearly opposite the vocabulary word.

1. discredit   a) doubt   b) trust   c) mistrust   d) lesson
2. adjacent   a) nearby   b) added on   c) distant   d) bordering
3. suppress   a) hold down   b) subdue   c) deflect   d) release
4. aloof   a) remote   b) involved   c) muddled   d) distant
5. vitality   a) weakness   b) vigor   c) strength   d) scheme
6. dispense   a) disband   b) please   c) scatter   d) collect

lesson 78

compel ▪ essence

compel (v) (kəm-ˈpel)

ORIGIN: Latin *com* (with) + *pellere* (to push drive)

MEANING: To drive or urge by using physical force, moral or social pressure, or logical necessity

CONTEXT: "Estelle was *compelled* to change her behavior because of the disapproval of her classmates."

SYNONYMS: force, impel, drive

OTHER FORMS: compellable (adj.), compelling (adj.), compellingly (adv.)

essence (n) (ˈes-n[t]s)

ORIGIN: Latin *esse* (to be)

MEANING: The most important property that makes a thing what it is

CONTEXT: "The *essence* of his speech was that all persons should have equal opportunities for employment."

SYNONYMS: substance, meaning, reality, core

OTHER FORMS: essential (adj.), essentialness (n.)

A. Focus on Meaning

Match each word with its synonym by writing the proper letter in the blank.

1. compel _____
2. essence _____
3. bigotry _____
4. contemplate _____
5. essential _____
6. compelling _____

a) necessary   b) ponder   c) core   d) force   e) driving   f) intolerance

B. Words in Context

Supply the proper form of the most appropriate vocabulary word.

| chafe   compel   essence   instigate   wrath |

1. Careful planning is a(n) _____ part of many jobs.

2. After fighting in the jungle for several days and suffering heavy casualties, the troops were finally _____ to withdraw into the highlands.

3. Ancient religious priests held that one might be spared the _____ vengeance of the gods if one offered sacrifices to them.

4. The FBI offered evidence that the riot was _____ by agitators who wished to discredit the government.

5. The captain was _____ to alter the ship's course to avoid a tropical storm that was advancing up the coast.

6. Many manufacturers of powdered breakfast drinks claim that the have captured the _____ of fresh fruit in their products.

7. Justin's new shoes were so stiff that they _____ his heals the first time he wore them.

lesson 79

comprehend ▪ pretense

comprehend (v)	(ˌkom-pri-ˈhend)	
ORIGIN:	Latin *com* (with, together) + *prehendere* (to grasp)	
MEANING:	To understand the nature or the meaning of something	
CONTEXT:	"He could not *comprehend* the instructions until I explained them step by step."	
SYNONYMS:	perceive, grasp, understand, fathom	
ANTONYMS:	misperceive, misunderstand	
OTHER FORMS:	comprehensive (adj.), comprehension (n.)	

pretense (n)	(ˈprē-ˌten[t]s)	
ORIGIN:	Latin *praetendere* (to pretend)	
MEANING:	A false rather than a real intention or purpose; a false show	
CONTEXT:	"My illness was a *pretense* to get out of school."	
SYNONYMS:	sham, pretext, show, ostentation, affectation	
ANTONYMS:	truth, sincerity, simpleness, naturalness, humility, unpretentiousness	
OTHER FORMS:	pretentious (adj.), pretension (n.)	

A. Focus on Meaning

Circle the letter of the best meaning for each vocabulary word.

1. comprehend: a) pretend b) predict c) raise up d) understand

2. pretense: a) false show b) fun c) vacuum d) package

3. compel: a) force b) immigrate c) complain d) plot

4. comprehend: a) perceive b) approve c) communicate d) conspire

5. pretense: a) affectation b) humility c) agony d) love

6. essence: a) odor b) load c) ecstasy d) substance

B. Words in Context

Supply the proper form of the most appropriate vocabulary word.

> bigotry   comprehend   contemplate   etiquette   grapple   pretense

1. Trudy's _____ in reading is very good, but her speed is not.

2. Experienced chess players never make split-second decisions but instead thoughtfully _____ each possibility before choosing their next moves.

3. It is _____ of Willie to parade up and down, leading his pure-bred collie in front of those boys whose dogs are mongrels.

4. Religious and racial intolerances, as well as other forms of _____, could be eliminated if tolerance and respect were emphasized in schools.

5. The spy attended the cabinet meeting under false _____.

6. The two Olympic wrestlers _____ with each other without either taking a fall.

7. At the formal dinner Robert was not sure of the _____. Which fork should he use first?

8. "I find it hard to _____," said Robin, "why you don't want to go to college."

lesson 80

combustion ▪ tedious

combustion (n) (kəm-ˈbəs-chən)

ORIGIN:	Latin *comburere* (to burn up)
MEANING:	The process of burning
CONTEXT:	"The gas engine gets its power from the *combustion* of the gasoline vapor."
SYNONYMS:	incineration, inflammation, burning
ANTONYMS:	cooling
OTHER FORMS:	combustive (adj.) combustible (adj.), combustibility (n.)

tedious (adj) (ˈtēd-ē-əs)

ORIGIN:	Latin *taedium* (irksome)
MEANING:	Tiresome because of dullness or length
CONTEXT:	"I was bored and exhausted by that *tedious* lecture on the works of Edgar Allan Poe."
SYNONYMS:	tiresome, boring, monotonous, dull, dry
ANTONYMS:	stimulating, amusing, entertaining, sparkling
OTHER FORMS:	tedium (n.)

A. Focus on Meaning

Circle the letter of the word in each group that does not belong.

1. a) combustion   b) burning   c) inflammation   d) cooling

2. a) tedious   b) tiresome   c) dull   d) entertaining

3. a) comprehend   b) know   c) perceive   d) exclude

4. a) pretense   b) humility   c) sham   d) pretext

5. a) combustion   b) burning   c) combat   d) incineration

B. Words in Context

Supply the proper form of the most appropriate vocabulary word.

combustion	comprehend	contemplate	essence	pretense	tedious

1. The fire in the old barn was caused by the spontaneous _____ of the tightly packed hay.

2. Shelling hickory nuts is _____ work, but the results are well worth the effort.

3. The _____ of a democracy is equal treatment of all persons regardless of race, color, religious belief, or ethnic origin.

4. Steve's _____ of liking Jessica's pudding was made to make her feel good.

5. Brian doesn't need to leave the room; he is too young to _____ what you are saying.

6. After _____ about a science fair project for a week, Naomi decided on magnetism.

7. At first I had a difficult time _____ algebra, but now it all makes sense to me.

8. Practicing foul shots for hours is _____, but pays off in the games.

LESSONS 61–80

For each numbered word choose the word or phrase that is closest in meaning to the vocabulary word. Write the letter for the word on the line provided

1. gait   a) rub   b) gain   1. _____
    c) pace   d) divert

2. bigotry   a) tolerance   b) open-mindedness   2. _____
    c) intolerance   d) strength

3. curtail   a) enlarge   b) lessen   3. _____
    c) increase   d) fumble

4. conspire   a) plot   b) confound   4. _____
    c) inspire   d) force

5. integrity   a) duplicity   b) sharpness   5. _____
    c) boredom   d) honesty

6. instigate   a) delay   b) amuse   6. _____
    c) start   d) collect

7. adjacent   a) bordering   b) distant   7. _____
    c) removed   d) added to

8. indifferent   a) concerned   b) unconcerned   8. _____
    c) contrived   d) committed

9. harass   a) befriend   b) support   9. _____
    c) turn aside   d) pester

10. vitality   a) robustness   b) weakness   10. _____
    c) virtue   d) healthy

11. advocate   a) disapprove   b) support   11. _____
    c) oppose   d) contrive

12. grope   a) grumble   b) force   12. _____
    c) fumble   d) grasp

13. divert   a) shorten   b) bother   13. _____
    c) fathom   d) turn aside

14. whet   a) dull   b) stimulate   14. _____
    c) satisfy   d) rage

15. suppress   a) subdue   b) release   15. _____
    c) broadcast   d) force

16. grapple   a) gather   b) pretend   16. _____
    c) incite   d) struggle

17. maze   a) corn   b) labyrinth   17. _____
    c) sham   d) fire

18. aloof   a) committed   b) involved   18. _____
    c) remote   d) bored

19. wrath   a) reason   b) joy   19. _____
    c) pretension   d) rage

20. chafe   a) irritate   b) please   20. _____
    c) soothe   d) inflame

Test Tips

Some tests - similar to Exercise B in this book - ask you to select the best word or words to complete a sentence. Before answering, read each choice carefully and eliminate the items that are clearly incorrect. Also be sure look for clues to the overall meaning of the sentence. Then try the possible answers in the sentence before choosing the best answer.

Practice: On the line provided write the word that best completes the meaning of the sentence.

1. After the last out was made in the baseball game the crowd _____ rapidly.

    (a) dispersed   (b) gathered

    (c) cheered   (d) walked

2. People who have trouble sleeping may have _____.

    (a) dreams   (b) indigestion

    (c) insomnia   (d) complexes

3. I always have a difficult time _____ what Elijah says.

    (a) hearing   (b) knowing

    (c) caring   (d) comprehending

lesson 81

mono- ▪ hemi-

mono- (prefix)

ORIGIN: Greek *monos* (alone)

MEANING: One, single, or alone

CONTEXT: "*mono*plane"

NOTE: You will also want to learn uni, the Latin word that means "one" or "single," as in united.

hemi- (prefix)

ORIGIN: Greek *hemi* (half)

MEANING: Half

CONTEXT: "*hemi*sphere"

OTHER FORMS: semi- (semicircle), demi- (demitasse)

A. Focus on Meaning

In each of the italicized words below, underline the word part that you have learned. Then, using your knowledge of the meaning of the word part, circle the letter of the best meaning for the italicized word.

1. *semiannual* visit: a) once a year   b) twice a year   c) infrequent   d) secret

2. a dazzling *spectrum*:   a) phenomenon   b) promise
   c) visible band of colors   d) prism

3. *monotonous* scenery: a) attractive   b) uniform
   c) consisting of mountains   d) stimulating

4. sipped their *demitasse*:   a) lemonade   b) alcoholic drinks
   c) small cups of coffee   d) large mugs of coffee

5. the *tensile* strength of linen: a) great   b) little   c) stretched out   d) woven

6. Col. Klink's *monocle*:   a) eyeglasses   b) cane   c) hearing aid   d) glass for one eye

7. afflicted with *hemialgia*:   a) bad vision   b) tuberculosis
   c) pain in half the body   d) color blindness

B. REVIEW

Match the correct definition to each vocabulary word. Write the letter of the definition on the line.

_____ 1. bigotry   a. force

_____ 2. comprehend   b. tiresome

_____ 3. pretense   c. core

_____ 4. contemplate   d. intolerance

_____ 5. tedious   e. study

_____ 6. compel   f. understand

_____ 7. essence   g. ostentation

_____ 8. combustion   h. incineration

consecrate ▪ trend

consecrate (v) (ˈkän[t]-sə-ˌkrāt)

ORIGIN: Latin *com* (with) + *sacrare* (to hallow)

MEANING: To devote to a purpose with deep dedication and solemnity; to make or declare sacred

CONTEXT: "Dr. Ed's life was *consecrated* to the service of humanity through the practice of medicine."

SYNONYMS: devote, dedicate, hallow, venerate

ANTONYM: desecrate

OTHER FORMS: consecration (n.), consecrative (adj.)

NOTE: Do not confuse with *concentrate*, which means "to gather" or "to collect together."

trend (n) (trend)

ORIGIN: Old English *trendan* (to turn, revolve)

MEANING: The general course or prevailing direction of events, preferences, styles, or behavior

CONTEXT: "The *trend* in education is to make preschool a part of the public school system-compulsory for all four year olds."

SYNONYMS: tendency, course, direction, style, vogue, mode

A. Focus on Meaning

Match each word with its synonym by writing the proper letter in the blank.

1. consecrate _____
2. trend _____
3. combustion _____
4. consecration _____
5. tedious _____
6. adjacent _____

a) burning   b) devote   c) tendency   d) tiresome   e) dedication   f) nearby

B. Words in Context

Supply the proper form of the most appropriate vocabulary word.

compel   consecrate   pretense   trend

1. The job of stock-market research experts involves analyzing business _____ and making economic predictions for investors.

2. Workers are upset over the _____ toward automation and the loss of jobs.

3. Liz and Eleanor got by with the _____ that they were sisters until their teacher visited Eleanor's home unexpectedly.

4. I feel _____ to attend the lecture because I was the one who suggested that we invite an astronaut to speak at our school.

5. Jason has _____ his life to helping the Navajo and has gone to teach in their schools.

6. Florence Nightingale's _____ to the nursing profession was reflected in everything she said or did.

Shades of Meaning

- devote
- dedicate
- consecrate
- hallow

lesson 83

prudent ▪ err

prudent	(adj)	('prüd-nt)
ORIGIN:	Latin *prudens* (provident)	
MEANING:	Wise or wisely cautious in practical affairs	
CONTEXT:	"Because of her *prudent* handling of her money, she was able to meet her obligations and still save."	
SYNONYMS:	discreet, wise, sensible	
ANTONYMS:	indiscreet, unwise	
OTHER FORMS:	prudence (n.), prudential (adj.), prudently (adv.)	

err	(v)	(e[ə]r)
ORIGIN:	Latin *errare* (go astray)	
MEANING:	To make a mistake, to violate an accepted standard of conduct	
CONTEXT:	"The fact that Tim *erred* once does not mean that he will make the mistake again."	
SYNONYMS:	stray, misjudge, blunder	
OTHER FORM:	errant (adj. meaning "wandering")	

A. Focus on Meaning

Circle the letter of the best meaning for each vocabulary word.

1. prudent: a) fruitful   b) sensible   c) weak   d) courageous
2. err: a) misjudge   b) inflate   c) fertilize   d) cut
3. consecrate: a) plot   b) implore   c) venerate   d) rave
4. trend: a) embroidery   b) tendency   c) ornament   d) shawl
5. prudently: a) wisely   b) expensively   c) angrily   d) humorously
6. errant: a) timely   b) content   c) wandering   d) relative

B. Words in Context

Supply the proper form of the most appropriate vocabulary word.

combustion	err	prudent	tedious

1. When traveling through the desert, it is _____ to carry a can of water in case one's car breaks down.
2. The teacher, realizing that he had _____ in calculating the grades, changed Bernie's C to a B.
3. Arthur flopped down on the bed as soon as he came in from an exhausting day of _____, monotonous work on the assembly line.
4. Denny revealed his lack of _____ when he left the keys in his unlocked car.
5. Cleaning fluid should never be used near an open flame because it is highly _____.

C. Antonyms

Circle the letter of the word whose meaning is most nearly opposite the vocabulary word.

1. integrity   a) virtue   b) honor   c) dishonesty   d) tolerance
2. tedious   a) boring   b) stimulating   c) monotonous   c) fresh
3. chafe   a) soothe   b) irritate   c) scrape   d) gravitate
4. pretense   a) affectation   b) sham   c) silliness   d) sincerity
5. consecrate   a) hallow   b) dedicate   c) desecrate   d) abandon
6. bigotry   a) tolerance   b) dogmatism   c) wisdom   d) truth

quench ▪ congestion

quench	(v)	(kwench)
ORIGIN:	Old English *civencan* (to extinguish)	
MEANING:	To put out, to satisfy, to inhibit	
CONTEXT:	"Nothing *quenches* my thirst like a tall glass of iced tea.	
SYNONYMS:	destroy, slake subdue extinguish, allay	
OTHER FORMS:	quenchable (adj.), unquenchable (adj.), quenchless (adj.)	

congestion	(n)	(kən-ˈjes[h]-chən)
ORIGIN:	Latin *com* (with, together) + *gerere* (to bring)	
MEANING:	Overcrowding in a small or narrow space	
CONTEXT:	"When the football game is over and the crowd begins to leave, the *congestion* in the streets slows traffic to a snail's pace.	
SYNONYM:	overcrowding	
ANTONYMS:	spaciousness, roominess	
OTHER FORM:	congest (v.)	

A. Focus on Meaning

Circle the letter of the best meaning for each vocabulary word.

1. quench: a) put out   b) explode   c) implore   d) quest

2. congestion: a) roominess   b) vacancy   c) overcrowding   d) illness

3. prudent: a) prudish   b) foolish   c) wise   d) careless

4. quench: a) wrench   b) help   c) start   d) extinguish

5. err: a) earn   b) blunder   c) listen   d) correct

6. trend: a) vogue   b) road   c) flight   d) trip

B. Words in Context

Supply the proper form of the most appropriate vocabulary word.

compel	comprehend	congestion	consecrate	err	essence	quench	trend

1. I developed a(n) _____ thirst driving through the arid desert.

2. The energy shortage has accelerated the _____ toward wind and solar power.

3. The _____ of the bread and the wine is an integral part of the Roman Catholic communion service.

4. The _____ in the corridors is a result of the unexpected early dismissal of classes.

5. During the basketball tournament, the parking lot was so _____ that one could scarcely walk through it.

6. Mr. Gomez told the class, "No one can _____ you to work hard in school, but I find it difficult to _____ why anyone would not use this time to become all that they can possibly be."

7. Do you know the old saying, "To _____ is human but to forgive is divine?"

8. Eve reminded everyone that it is absolutely _____ to be at the station by 7:45 A.M. because the train leaves at 7:53 A.M. sharp.

lesson 85

-gen- ■ -corp-

-gen-	(root)
ORIGIN:	Latin *genus* (birth)
MEANING:	Birth
CONTEXT:	"*gen*erate"

-corp-	(root)
ORIGIN:	Latin *corpus* (body)
MEANING:	Body
CONTEXT:	"*Corp*se"
OTHER FORM:	-torpor- (corporal)

A. Focus on Meaning

In each of the italicized words below, underline the word parts that you have learned. Then, using your knowledge of the meanings of the word parts, circle the letter of the best meaning for the italicized word. (For some words there may be only one word part.)

1. red *corpuscles* in the blood:　a) drops of poison　　b) germs
　　　　　　　　　　　　　　c) traces of drugs　　d) minute cells of the body

2. *corporal* punishment:　a) severe　　b) ending life, such as electrocution
　　　　　　　　　　c) inflicted by a soldier　　d) directed against the body, such as whipping

3. an *incompatible* couple:　a) getting along well　　b) not getting along
　　　　　　　　　　　c) unique　　d) friendly

4. *engendered* by hatred:　a) divided　　b) given birth to　　c) made worse　　d) united

5. the *progeny* of a great man:　a) early education　　b) children　　c) death　　d) acts

6. a *corpulent* man:　a) compulsive　　b) large-bodied　　c) long-legged　　d) bighearted

7. the *genesis* of the world:　a) goodness　　b) meanness　　c) creation　　d) purpose

B. REVIEW

Match the correct definition to each vocabulary word. Write the letter of the definition on the line.

_____ 1. consecrate　　　　a. torment

_____ 2. harass　　　　　　b. understand

_____ 3. congestion　　　　c. overcrowding

_____ 4. trend　　　　　　d. start

_____ 5. conspire　　　　　e. hallow

_____ 6. prudent　　　　　f. scheme

_____ 7. comprehend　　　g. discreet

_____ 8. instigate　　　　　h. tendency

lesson 86

agitate ▪ widespread

agitate (v) (ˈaj-ə-tāt)

ORIGIN: Latin *agere* (to drive)

MEANING: To move, force, shake, or rouse into brisk, sometimes violent, motion or action

CONTEXT: "The crowd was *agitated* by several impassioned speakers to the point that they began a march to City Hall to protest the increase in taxes."

SYNONYMS: disturb, trouble, stir, arouse, excite

ANTONYMS: calm, soothe

OTHER FORMS: agitation (n.), agitator (n.), agitative (adj.)

widespread (adj) (ˈwīd-ˈspred)

ORIGIN: Old English *wid* (gone apart) + spraedon (to sprinkle)

MEANING: Spread over or occupying a wide space or many places

CONTEXT: "*Widespread* poverty is a big problem confronting the entire country."

SYNONYMS: extensive, far-reaching, dispersed, boundless

ANTONYMS: confined, restricted, limited

OTHER FORM: widespreading (adj.)

A. Focus on Meaning

Circle the letter of the best meaning for each vocabulary word.

1. agitate: a) disturb   b) calm   c) reduce   d) calculate

2. widespread: a) limited   b) occasional   c) extensive   d) infrequent

3. quench: a) create   b) propel   c) satisfy   d) inhabit

4. congest: a) monopolize   b) cough   c) bluster   d) crowd

5. agitate: a) soothe   b) stir   c) steal   d) ponder

B. Words in Context

Supply the proper form of the most appropriate vocabulary word.

agitate	combustion	err	tedious	trend	widespread

1. Ralph Nader became well known when he _____ for laws to improve automobile safety.

2. The pilot _____ when he computed the amount of fuel necessary for the flight and consequently was forced to land fifty miles from his destination.

3. When the harvest is poor in India, famine is _____.

4. Many citizens, both black and white, are _____ to reorganize the school system.

5. _____ discontent over many issues will continue to affect many communities until conditions are improved.

6. Cutting the lawn can be very _____, especially in the spring when the grass grows rapidly.

7. The latest _____ _____ in fashion has my grandfather very upset.

8. Because of the danger from fire or explosions, _____ materials can no longer be moved down Main Street by truck.

lesson 87

scoff ▪ graft

scoff   (v)   (skảf)

ORIGIN: Old Norse *shof* (a taunt)

MEANING: To treat with contempt, show contempt for, or scorn by acts or by language that mocks and ridicules

CONTEXT: "Don't *scoff* at the coach's training rules; his team is always in good condition and rarely loses a game."

SYNONYMS: jeer, sneer, deride, ridicule

OTHER FORMS: scoffer (n.), scoffingly (adv.)

graft   (n)   (graft)

ORIGIN: Probably from Greek *graphein* (to write)

MEANING: Gain or advantage through dishonest, unfair, or sordid means—especially through misusing one's position or influence in business or in government

CONTEXT: "The city's treasurer was suspected of *graft* when it was learned that her brother's company was given a contract for all sewer pipe bought by the city."

SYNONYMS: corruption, swindling

A. Focus on Meaning

Match each word with its synonym by writing the proper letter in the blank.

1. scoff _____
2. graft _____
3. agitate _____
4. widespread _____
5. scoffingly _____
6. gait _____

a) excite   b) ridicule   c) extensive   d) way of walking   e) jeeringly   f) corruption

B. Words in Context

Supply the proper form of the most appropriate vocabulary word.

congestion   consecrate   graft   prudent   quench   scoff

1. Many people _____ at the idea of putting a person on the moon, but they were proved wrong in July 1969.

2. Some politicians feel that _____ in government is an acceptable way of supplementing their low salaries.

3. The _____ on downtown streets during the daily rush hour is so bad that the city council is considering the construction of a mass transit system.

4. My father claims that nothing _____ his thirst on a hot summer day as much as fruit juice.

5. The reporter was praised for her exposure of _____ on the part of immigration officials.

6. Those that _____ at Robert Fulton's first steamboat would surely be astonished by the huge steamships of today.

7. It is _____ to make a checklist of all the things you will need for a camping trip.

8. The new chapel at our church was _____ last Saturday.

lesson 88

consecutive ▪ alternate

consecutive (adj)	(kən-ˈsek-[y]ət-iv)		**alternate** (adj)	(ˈȯl-tər-nət)	

consecutive (adj) (kən-ˈsek-[y]ət-iv)

ORIGIN: Latin *consequi* (to follow after)

MEANING: Following one after the other in uninterrupted order

CONTEXT: "Franklin Roosevelt was the first president to serve three *consecutive* terms."

SYNONYMS: successive continuous

ANTONYMS: disjoined, discontinuous

OTHER FORMS: consecutively (adv.), consecutiveness (n.)

alternate (adj) (ˈȯl-tər-nət)

ORIGIN: Latin *alternare* (to do by turns)

MEANING: Occurring or succeeding by turns, interchanging repeatedly and regularly with one another

CONTEXT: "Apply *alternate* compresses, cold then hot, to the ankle."

SYNONYM: intermittent

ANTONYM: continuous

OTHER FORMS: alternate (v.), alternately (adv.), alternation (n.)

A. Focus on Meaning

Circle the letter of the best meaning for each vocabulary word.

1. consecutive: a) lively   b) poetic   c) successive   d) autobiographical

2. alternate: a) intermittent   b) changeless   c) tragic   d) harmful

3. graft: a) carving   b) grammar   c) corruption   d) tone

4. scoff: a) praise   b) jeer   c) scream fearfully   d) wander

5. consecutive: a) joyful   b) emotional   c) executive   d) continuous

6. alternate: a) continue   b) replace   c) change back and forth   d) perform

B. Words in Context

Supply the proper form of the most appropriate vocabulary word.

agitate	alternate	congestion	consecutive	prudent	widespread

1. These three _____ lessons, four, five, and six, will be followed by a test.

2. The ninth grade will take _____ seats beginning with the first desk; the eighth grade, beginning with the second desk.

3. After four _____ nights of heavy rain, the river began to crest, and many people were forced to flee their homes ahead of the rising water.

4. This storm is _____, covering most of the Midwest, and is moving into the Southeast rapidly.

5. Mac, don't do anything to _____ your sister, for she is already disturbed enough over losing the opportunity to compete in the Olympic games.

6. Joyce and John cleaned up after the family dinner on _____ days of the week.

7. There are more and more cars and trucks on the roads every day. Sitting in traffic _____ has become the normal way of life for many people.

8. Roni and Rico _____ waited beneath the stands until the rain stopped at the ball park.

lesson 89

-fac- ▪ -gress-

-fac- (root)

ORIGIN: Latin *facere* (to make or do)

MEANING: To make or do

CONTEXT: "*fac*ulty"

OTHER FORMS: -fact- (manufacture), -fic- (efficacious), -fit- (benefit), -feet- (perfect), -fash- (fashion)

-gress- (root)

ORIGIN: Latin *gradi* (to go)

MEANING: To go, to step

CONTEXT: "pro*gress*"

OTHER FORM: -grad- (graduate)

A. Focus on Meaning

In each of the italicized words below, underline the word part that you have learned. Then, using your knowledge of the meaning of the word part, circle the letter of the best meaning for the italicized word.

1. put into a *classification*: a) room with a teacher and other students
   b) category made separate from the rest   c) jail   d) lottery

2. startling *regression*: a) movement backward step by step   b) act of violence
   c) feelings of hostility   d) admission

3. *rectification* of the difficulty: a) process of making a situation more acceptable
   b) implication   c) disappearance   d) conclusion

4. a simple *monomial*: a) apparatus   b) algebraic expression having a single term
   c) solution   d) mechanism

5. a *gradual* decline: a) abrupt   b) slow, step by step   c) steep   d) tragic

6. a damaged *faculty*: a) industrial complex   b) front fender   c) ability to do d) lung

B. REVIEW

Match the correct definition to each vocabulary word. Write the letter of the definition on the line.

_____ 1. agitate   a. corruption

_____ 2. quench   b. burning

_____ 3. scoff   c. pester

_____ 4. combustion   d. disturb

_____ 5. widespread   e. intolerance

_____ 6. harass   f. ridicule

_____ 7. graft   g. extensive

_____ 8. bigotry   h. extinguish

lesson 90

compromise ▪ intrusion

compromise (v) (ˈkȧm-prə-mīz)

ORIGIN: Latin *compromittere* (to make a mutual promise)

MEANING: To settle or adjust differences by mutual concessions

CONTEXT: "Because the children wanted to vacation at the seashore and Father wanted to go to the mountains, Mother suggested that they *compromise* by spending half the time at each place."

SYNONYMS: adjust, mediate, arbitrate

OTHER FORM: compromise (n.)

intrusion (n) (in-ˈtrü-zhən)

ORIGIN: Latin *intrudere* (to thrust)

MEANING: To come or bring in without invitation or welcome

CONTEXT: "Your *intrusion* while I was talking with your sister was very rude."

SYNONYMS: interference, encroachment

OTHER FORMS: intrude (v.), intrusive (adj.)

A. Focus on Meaning

Circle the letter of the best meaning for each vocabulary word.

1. compromise: a) meet   b) combine   c) arbitrate   d) influence

2. intrude: a) enter when invited   b) enter without an invitation
   c) stay outside   d) run at a fast pace

3. consecutive: a) every other one   b) following one after the other
   c) selective   d) with success

4. compromise: a) mediate   b) promise help   c) understand   d) comprehend

5. alternate: a) one of one kind, then one of another   b) successive
   c) short   d) electrical

B. Words in Context

Supply the proper form of the most appropriate vocabulary word.

compromise	graft	intrude	quench	scoff

1. School may close unless the teachers and the school board can reach a(n) _____ on the terms of the new contract.

2. If you do not want your brother to _____ on your privacy, then you should respect his.

3. A(n) _____ was reached by the managers and the employees on the question of overtime pay.

4. Don't _____ at the idea of your sister being elected president of her class, for she is very friendly, well liked, and capable.

5. The use of cell phones is considered an unwelcome _____ in many public places.

6. The heavy rains of the thunderstorm _____ the forest fire in Fairfield County.

7. The present administration has worked hard to prevent any _____ on the part of government officials.

lesson 91

abide ▪ gracious

abide (v) (ə-ˈbīd)

ORIGIN:	Old English *bidan* (to remain)
MEANING 1:	To remain, continue, dwell
CONTEXT 1:	"The retired gardener *abides* in the little rooming house in the village."
MEANING 2:	To put up with, to tolerate
CONTEXT 2:	"I can't *abide* snobbish people."
SYNONYMS:	tarry, live, stay; bear, endure, accept
OTHER FORM:	abode (n. meaning "home")

gracious (adj) (ˈgrā-shəs)

ORIGIN:	Latin *gratia* (grace, thanks)
MEANING:	Showing kindness, courtesy, charm, good taste
CONTEXT:	"Anne, a *gracious* person, is always concerned about the comfort, feelings, and welfare of others."
SYNONYMS:	cordial, affable, genial, sociable
ANTONYMS:	graceless, ungracious
OTHER FORMS:	graciously (adv.), graciousness (n.)

A. Focus on Meaning

Circle the letter of the best meaning for each vocabulary word.

1. abide: a) endure b) care c) fear d) reject

2. gracious: a) mean b) energetic c) forceful d) thoughtful

3. compromise: a) conspire b) mediate c) meditate d) submit

4. intrusion: a) purpose b) encroachment c) expedition d) journey

5. consecutive: a) irresponsible b) successive c) intelligent d) harmful

B. Words in Context

Supply the proper form of the most appropriate vocabulary word.

abide consecutive gracious

1. _____ is a characteristic associated with diplomats.

2. "There are two things," said the boss, "that I simply cannot _____: tardiness and poor performance."

3. You will have three _____ days off from school because classes will be dismissed on Thursday afternoon.

4. A practice among some members of the animal kingdom is for different species to _____ together; for example, bees and mice may share a tree hole, and rattlesnakes often move in with prairie dogs.

Shades of Meaning
- gracious
- cordial
- affable
- genial
- sociable

lesson 92
turf ▪ genteel

turf (n) (tərf)

ORIGIN: Old English *turf* (tuft of grass)

MEANING: A layer of earth formed by grass and plant roots matted together

CONTEXT: "The football team practices on the old field because the *turf* on the new one is not yet thick enough to withstand much wear."

SYNONYM: sod

OTHER FORMS: turfless (adj.), turflike (adj.)

genteel (adj) (jen-ˈtē[ə]l)

ORIGIN: Latin *gentilis* (belonging to the same family, high born)

MEANING: Well bred or refined, belonging or suited to polite society

CONTEXT: "The *genteel* lady sat erect on her chair, talking in a firm but soft voice."

SYNONYMS: well bred, polite

ANTONYMS: impolite, boorish, coarse, vulgar

OTHER FORMS: genteelly (adv.), gentility (n.)

A. Focus on Meaning

Circle the letter of the best meaning for each vocabulary word.

1. turf: a) sod b) country c) base d) goal
2. genteel: a) uninvited b) resourceful c) well bred d) stubborn
3. abide: a) live b) testify c) forget d) shelter
4. genteelly: a) richly b) politely c) pretentiously d) ostentatiously
5. utensil: a) tool b) object of art c) prehistoric painting d) art form

B. Words in Context

Supply the proper form of the most appropriate vocabulary word.

| abide | alternate | compromise | genteel | intrusion | turf |

1. The fans took pieces of _____ from the field for souvenirs after the Mets won the World Series.
2. Mother coached us on correct behavior so that we would become models of _____ in time for the formal ball.
3. The British aristocracy engages in _____ activities such as playing croquet and fox hunting.
4. Years ago houses were made of pieces of _____ cut from the prairie and stacked together in much the same manner as brick is laid today.
5. A skunk _____ on our family's picnic and sent us dashing in all directions.
6. Frances is the sixth starter on the basketball team; she _____ at left guard with Alicia.
7. After days of arguing, Nora and Ted finally _____ on the date for the surprise party.
8. "If you refuse to _____ by all the rules of the game," warned the coach, "you will harm yourself and the team."

lesson 93

invincible ▪ sparse

invincible   (adj)   (in-ˈvin[t]-ˌsə-bəl)

ORIGIN: Latin *in* (not) + *vincere* (to conquer)

MEANING: That which cannot be overcome, subdued, or conquered

CONTEXT: "Everyone thought the high school football team was *invincible*, but they lost by one point last night."

SYNONYMS: indomitable, unconquerable, all-powerful, unyielding

ANTONYMS: conquerable, yielding, powerless

OTHER FORMS: invincibility (n.), invincibleness (n.), invincibly (adv.)

sparse   (adj)   (spȧrs)

ORIGIN: Latin *sparsus* (scattered)

MEANING: Not thick or dense, thin

CONTEXT: "Earl has such *sparse* hair that there is no doubt he will be bald by middle age."

SYNONYMS: scanty, meager, scattered, thin

ANTONYMS: abundant, bounteous, thick

OTHER FORMS: sparsely (adv.), sparseness (n.)

A. Focus on Meaning

Circle the letter of the word in each group that does not belong.

1. a) invincible   b) invisible   c) indomitable   d) unconquerable
2. a) sparse   b) scanty   c) meager   d) colorful
3. a) turf   b) sod   c) timber   d) grass
4. a) sparseness   b) meagerness   c) bounteousness   d) scantiness
5. a) invincible   b) all-powerful   c) unyielding   d) visible

B. Words in Context

Supply the proper form of the most appropriate vocabulary word.

> bigotry   genteel   invincible   sparse

1. As we traveled toward Yosemite National Park, the _____ desert vegetation gave way to luxurious stands of timber.
2. The apparent _____ of Farmington's football team is borne out by its record of twenty-nine straight wins and no losses.
3. The Ku Klux Klan has historically been an organization of _____ who have sought to prevent black people from taking their rightful place in society.
4. Although Lee Ann was accustomed to _____ living, she adjusted quite readily to the rough, often crude conditions under which she lived as a Peace Corp volunteer.
5. The _____ of the furnishings in the couple's apartment was barely noticeable because they had decorated the place so artfully.

C. Antonyms

Circle the letter of the word whose meaning is most nearly opposite the vocabulary word.

1. prudent   a) wise   b) sensible   c) devoted   d) indiscreet
2. genteel   a) friendly   b) vulgar   c) well-bred   d) polite
3. agitate   a) excite   b) disturb   c) soothe   d) break
4. consecutive   a) disjoined   b) successive   c) successful   d) continuous
5. congestion   a) overcrowding   b) extensive   c) boundless   d) roominess
6. gracious   a) gentle   b) benevolent   c) graceless   d) powerless

lesson 94

trans- ▪ circum-

trans- (prefix)

ORIGIN: Latin *trans* (across)

MEANING: Across

CONTEXT: "*trans*mit"

circum- (prefix)

ORIGIN: Latin *circus* (circle)

MEANING: Around

CONTEXT: "*circum*ference"

A. Focus on Meaning

In each of the italicized words below, underline the word parts that you have learned. Then, using your knowledge of the meanings of the word parts, circle the letter of the best meaning for the italicized word. (For some words there may be only one word part.)

1. a *transcontinental* railroad: a)charging high fares   b)stretching across the country   c)stopping in small towns   d) moving fast

2. *circumvent* the obstacle: a) cross   b) remove   c) go around   d) swim beyond

3. a line *transverse* to the first one: a) lying parallel   b) lying vertical   c) lying across   d) longer than

4. a *circumflex* artery: a) straight   b) large   c) bending around   d) running parallel

5. the study of *eugenics*: a) science of human relations   b) science of homemaking   c) science of improving children born to humans   d) science of improving plant life

6. *transpose* second and third letters of a word: a) erase   b) write more clearly   c) underline   d) change the places of

7. a *circumvascular* muscle: a) near a large blood vessel   b) near a small blood vessel   c) under a blood vessel   d) around a blood vessel

B. REVIEW

Match the correct definition to each vocabulary word. Write the letter of the definition on the line.

_____ 1. compromise   a) gentle

_____ 2. turf   b) adjust

_____ 3. conspire   c) sod

_____ 4. intrusion   d) plot

_____ 5. genteel   e) subdue

_____ 6. abide   f) interference

_____ 7. suppress   g) polite

_____ 8. gracious   h) bear

Lesson 94 • TRANS-/CIRCUM- **105**

lesson 95

data ▪ traverse

data   (n)   ('dāt-ə)

ORIGIN: Latin *datus* (a thing given)

MEANING: Factual information used as a basis for calculation, reasoning, or discussion

CONTEXT: "You should collect all *data* possible on your topic before you start writing the report."

SYNONYMS: facts, statistics, information

traverse   (v)   ('tra-vərs)

ORIGIN: Latin *traps* (across) + *vertere* (to turn)

MEANING: To go to and fro, to pass over, along, up and down

CONTEXT: "The early pioneers had to look for a place where they could *traverse* streams, rivers, mountains, and chasms."

SYNONYMS: ford, swim, cross, pass, bridge

OTHER FORMS: traversable (adj.), traversal (n.)

A. Focus on Meaning

Match each word with its synonym by writing the proper letter in the blank.

1. data _____   2. traverse_____   3. invincible_____

4. sparse _____   5. aloof _____   6. foul   _____

a) detached   b) unconquerable   c) loathsome   d) facts   e) thin   f) cross

B. Words in Context

Supply the proper form of the most appropriate vocabulary word.

data   foster   genteel   gracious   intrusion   traverse

1. He was a member of a(n) _____, old-fashioned family who lived quietly on their country estate.

2. Terry searched through the library for _____ on the effects of arsenic poisoning but was able to find nothing recently published.

3. The sociologists interviewed several hundred inhabitants of the small town and used this collection of _____ to compile an interesting report.

4. Johnny Appleseed _____ Ohio, planting apple trees as he went across the state.

5. A kindly approach to their dog is one way to (promote) _____ friendship with new neighbors.

6. Although they did not establish permanent homes in this part of the state, the Iroquois often _____ the area to hunt game.

7. Last night there was one _____ after another that kept me from finishing my book.

8. The camp counselor was so _____ that she made the newcomers feel right at home.

lesson 96
trivial ▪ garland

trivial (adj) (ˈtriv-ē-əl)

ORIGIN: Latin *trivialis* (commonplace)

MEANING: Ordinary, commonplace, of little worth

CONTEXT: "Don't bother her with such *trivial* matters as when and where to have the car washed; use your own judgment."

SYNONYMS: insignificant, unimportant, immaterial, small, petty, paltry, trifling

ANTONYMS: significant, worthwhile, important

OTHER FORMS: triviality (n.) trivia (n.)

garland (n) (ˈgȧr-lənd)

ORIGIN: Middle French *garlande* (wreath of flowers)

MEANING: A wreath or rope of leaves or flowers

CONTEXT: "A *garland* of flowers was hung around the neck of the winning horse."

SYNONYMS: festoon, wreath, lei, ornament

A. Focus on Meaning

Circle the letter of the best meaning for each vocabulary word.

1. trivial: a) worthless b) unpleasant c) interesting d) foreign

2. garland: a) favor b) field c) wreath d) desert

3. data: a) falsehoods b) statistics c) graphs d) equations

4. traverse: a) transcribe b) cross c) slide d) gallop

5. garland: a) grand piano b) concert hall c) lei d) gambler

B. Words in Context

Supply the proper form of the most appropriate vocabulary word.

agitate   garland   genteel   invincible   sparse   trivial

1. When you disembark in Honolulu, expect your friends to put a(n) _____ of flowers, called a lei, about your neck.

2. The residents on our block are always _____ for more police protection.

3. I find Joshua trees, part of the _____ vegetation in the desert in California, interesting and strangely beautiful.

4. The seemingly _____ army of Napoleon was defeated at the Battle of Waterloo in June 1815.

5. As children we wove _____ from clover and wild flowers.

6. "Jose, don't give me any of your _____ excuses for not mowing the lawn today."

7. The ten-year-old Allen twins were so _____ that we told their parents that we would gladly babysit for them any time.

8. "All that she talks about," Arlene proclaimed, " is a lot of _____."

lesson 97

consolidate ▪ radical

consolidate (v) (kən-ˈsȧl-ə-ˌdāt)

ORIGIN: Latin *com* (with, together) + *solidare* (to make solid)

MEANING: To join or bring together into a whole

CONTEXT: "The three small schools were *consolidated* into one large county high school."

SYNONYMS: join, unite, combine, merge, pool

ANTONYMS: divide, separate

OTHER FORM: consolidation (n.)

radical (adj) (ˈrad-i-kəl)

ORIGIN: Latin *radix* (root)

MEANING: Favoring or tending to make extreme changes in existing views, conditions, habits, or institutions

CONTEXT: "A group of *radical* students was behind the militant action that climaxed in the burning of the embassy."

SYNONYMS: drastic, immoderate, extreme, fanatical

ANTONYM: moderate

OTHER FORMS: radicalness (n.), radically (adv.), radicalism (n.)

A. Focus on Meaning

Circle the letter of the best meaning for each vocabulary word.

1. consolidate: a) divert   b) split   c) merge   d) rescue

2. radical: a) immoderate   b) unconstitutional   c) tyrannical   d) uninterrupted

3. trivial: a) large in size   b) insignificant   c) domestic   d) exclusive

4. consolidation: a) combination   b) prevention   c) addition of unrelated elements   d) compromise

5. garland: a) festival   b) loom   c) halo   d) wreath

6. radicalness: a) moderation   b) conservatism   c) chaos   d) extremeness

B. Words in Context

Supply the proper form of the most appropriate vocabulary word.

consolidate	data	invincible	sparse	radical	traverse

1. The _____ of the two radical groups into one gave them more members than the conservative organization.

2. One climber fell attempting to _____ the north face of Grand Teton Mountain.

3. In Columbus's time, his proposed voyage to find a new route to India was called _____.

4. Rather than buying two cheap stereos, Mark and Sam decided to _____ their resources and buy one high-quality model.

5. The _____ right-wing politicians were sure that their candidate for governor was _____.

6. In 1990 the _____ was still too _____ for scientists to be fairly certain that global warming was really happening.

7. To provide more educational choices for students, several of the smaller school systems were _____.

lesson 98

pre- ∎ post-

pre-	(prefix)	**post-**	(prefix)
ORIGIN:	Latin *prae* (before)	ORIGIN:	Latin *post* (behind, after)
MEANING:	Before, ahead of time, prior to, in front of	MEANING:	After or later
CONTEXT:	"*pre*dict"	CONTEXT:	"*post*paid"
NOTE:	You will also want to learn *ante-*, a Latin prefix meaning "before," as in *ante*cedent. Be careful, though, not to confuse *ante-* with *anti-*, a Greek root meaning "against," as in *anti*aircraft.		

A. Focus on Meaning

In each of the italicized words below, underline the word parts that you have learned. Then, using your knowledge of the meanings of the word parts, circle the letter of the best meaning for the italicized word. (For some words there may be only one word part.)

1. a *precursor* of spring: a) follower b) forerunner c) lover d) hater

2. *postpone* the meeting: a) announce ahead of time b) plan c) put off until later d) attend

3. *prevent* a disaster: a) help to occur b) stop before it occurs c) live through d) explain

4. *transgress* the law: a) obey b) explain c) go beyond the rules d) change the limits

5. *posthumous* award for bravery: a) given before death b) given after death c) given at death d) given because of death

6. *premature* baby: a) beautiful b) born late c) born ahead of time d) heavy

7. *transition* from a monarchy to a democracy: a) a long way b) a change c) a telegram d) a message

B. REVIEW

Match the correct definition to each vocabulary word. Write the letter of the definition on the line.

_____ 1. trivial   a. wreath

_____ 2. compel   b. cross

_____ 3. garland   c. sham

_____ 4. pretense   d. enthusiastic

_____ 5. data   e. insignificant

_____ 6. traverse   f. statistics

_____ 7. ardent   g. study

_____ 8. contemplate   h. force

lesson 99

strife ■ presume

strife   (n)   (strīf)

ORIGIN:	Old French *estri* (to fight)
MEANING:	Bitter and sometimes violent conflict
CONTEXT:	"The Arab-Israeli *controversy* has generated such strife that war has erupted several times since 1948."
SYNONYMS:	disagreement, conflict, opposition, fight
ANTONYM:	peace

presume   (v)   (pri-´züm)

ORIGIN:	Late Latin *prae* (before) + *sumere* (to take)
MEANING:	To suppose, without proof, to be true
CONTEXT:	"Our laws *presumes* that all persons charged with crimes are innocent until they are proved guilty."
SYNONYMS:	assume, presuppose
OTHER FORMS:	presumably (adv.), presumable (adj.), presumption (n.)

A. Focus on Meaning

Circle the letter of the best meaning for each vocabulary word.

1. strife: a) strike   b) blow   c) conflict   d) enjoyment

2. presume: a) hope   b) summon   c) presuppose   d) assure

3. consolidate: a) solve   b) unite   c) divide   d) celebrate

4. radical: a) racial   b) extreme   c) tolerant   d) impartial

5. presume: a) postpone   b) pretend   c) wish   d) assume

B. Words in Context

Supply the proper form of the most appropriate vocabulary word.

consolidate	garland	presume	strife	trivial

1. Because Mary often failed to turn in her homework, Mrs. Martin _____ that she was lazy, not knowing that she had to work six hours a day after school to help her family.

2. The armed _____ that began in 1980 between Afghan guerrillas and Soviet troops threatened the security of the countries in the region of the Persian Gulf.

3. As part of the Mother's Day ceremony in our community, a(n) _____ of roses was placed around the neck of the oldest mother present.

4. After several months of _____, the electrical workers and General Electronics finally settled their differences to the satisfaction of both parties.

5. I was enraged that Ted _____ that he could borrow my tennis racket without asking.

6. To save money, the company _____ their three offices into one.

7. Emma always keeps her mind on the big picture and ignores the _____ details.

8. Maria just _____ that Alec would remember to bring the tickets for the game.

lesson 100

tousle ▪ novel

tousle	(v)	(ˈtaů-zəl)
ORIGIN:	Middle English *touselen* (to touse, pull)	
MEANING:	To disarrange, dishevel, or tangle	
CONTEXT:	"As we walked down the street, the wind whipped our skirts about us and *tousled* our hair."	
SYNONYM:	rumple	
ANTONYM:	smoothe	
OTHER FORM:	tousled (adj.)	

novel	(adj)	(ˈnȧv-əl)
ORIGIN:	Latin *nouellus* (fresh, young, new)	
MEANING:	New and different from any other thing	
CONTEXT:	"That was a *novel* idea for a skit, one that I had never heard of before. "	
SYNONYMS:	new, modern, original, fresh	
ANTONYMS:	traditional, customary, usual, same	
OTHER FORM:	novelty (n.)	

A. Focus on Meaning

Match each word with its synonym by writing the proper letter in the blank.

1. tousle _____
2. novel _____
3. strife _____
4. clamber_____
5. presume_____
6. novelty_____

a) newness   b) presuppose   c) rumple   d) unique   e) scramble   f) conflict

B. Words in Context

Supply the proper form of the most appropriate vocabulary word.

consolidate   novel   tousle

1. My sister holds such _____ political views that she refuses to vote for any candidate that is in either of the two major political parties.

2. The _____ of the new toy will soon wear off, and your brother will let you play.

3. Grandmother always wore a nightcap so that her hair would not get _____ while she slept.

4. The two companies _____ their holdings and became a large corporation.

5. The Green Tree, a new gift shop in town, has many _____ gift items not found elsewhere.

6. "Don't play in the leaves and _____ your hair and clothes before we go to church, ordered Mother.

Shades of Meaning

- novel
- new
- modern
- original
- fresh

LESSONS 81–100

For each numbered word choose the word or phrase that is closest to the meaning of the vocabulary word. Write the letter for the word on the line provided.

1. gracious   (a) graceless   (b) grateful   1. _____
             (c) tolerant   (d) showing kindness

2. agitate   (a) disturb   (b) soothe   2. _____
             (c) calm   (d) forget

3. consecrate   (a) arouse   (b) endure   3. _____
             (c) dedicate   (d) desecrate

4. trivial   (a) important   (b) worthwhile   4. _____
             (c) insignificant   (d) unique

5. strife   (a) tousle   (b) conflict   5. _____
             (c) sneer   (d) arbitrate

6. prudent   (a) indiscreet   (b) excited   6. _____
             (c) bold   (d) sensible

7. quench   (a) overwhelm   (b) divide   7. _____
             (c) extinguish   (d) restrict

8. consolidate   (a) combine   (b) separate   8. _____
             (c) accept   (d) bring forth

9. compromise   (a) change   (b) arbitrate   9. _____
             (c) alternate   (d) stay

10. novel   (a) traditional   (b) customary   10. _____
             (c) published   (d) new

11. scoff   (a) swindle   (b) blunder   11. _____
             (c) ridicule   (d) praise

12. consecutive   (a) continuous   (b) disjoined   12. _____
             (c) execute   (d) postpone

13. data   (a) unique   (b) corruption   13. _____

              (c) information   (d) resources

14. radical   (a) moderate   (b) extreme   14. _____

              (c) political   (d) stylish

15. traverse   (a) transport   (b) carry   15. _____

              (c) stay   (d) cross

16. genteel   (a) vulgar   (b) friendly   16. _____

              (c) coarse   (d) polite

17. abide   (a) endure   (b) pass   17. _____

              (c) hide   (d) yield

18. trend   (a) tarry   (b) direction   18. _____

              (c) ornament   (d) accept

19. sparse   (a) thick   (b) abundant   19. _____

              (c) meager   (d) sensible

20. widespread   (a) limited   (b) confined   20. _____

              (c) extensive   (d) powerful

Test Tips

Some tests - similar to Exercise B in this book - ask you to select the best word or words to complete a sentence. Before answering, read each choice carefully and eliminate the items that are clearly incorrect. Also be sure look for clues to the overall meaning of the sentence. Then try the possible answers in the sentence before choosing the best answer.

Practice: On the line provided write the word that best completes the meaning of the sentence.

1. When traveling on the 4th of July expect long delays at the bridge because of _____.

         (a) sight seeing   (b) fireworks

         (c) road construction   (d) congestion

2. Larry's sudden _____ in the middle of the service disturbed everyone.

         (a) sleeping   (b) walking

         (c) intrusion   (d) smiling

3. I'm sorry I didn't ask but I just _____ you had a ride to the game.

         (a) guessed   (b) presumed

         (c) wished   (d) thought

lesson 101

abstract ▪ singe

abstract	(adj)	(ab-´strakt)

ORIGIN: Latin *abstrahere* (to draw from)

MEANING: Existing as an idea or a concept

CONTEXT: "Patriotism, honesty, and respect are *abstract* ideas."

SYNONYMS: intangible, conceptual

ANTONYMS: tangible concrete

OTHER FORMS: abstractly (adv.), abstractness (n.), abstraction (n.)

singe	(v)	(sinj)

ORIGIN: Old English *sengan* (to burn)

MEANING: To burn slightly (generally to remove fuzz, down, or hair by passing briefly over a flame)

CONTEXT: "When she bent over the campfire to put on more wood, she *singed* her bangs."

SYNONYMS: scorch, sear

A. Focus on Meaning

Circle the letter of the best meaning for each vocabulary word.

1. abstract: a) removed b) absent c) conceptual d) unintelligible

2. singe: a) sin b) cut c) scorch d) scatter

3. tousle: a) smoothe b) trim c) dishevel d) awaken

4. novel: a) fictional b) funny c) large d) new

5. abstract: a) contractual b) intangible c) true d) concrete

B. Words in Context

Supply the proper form for the most appropriate vocabulary word.

abstract	controversy	garland	presume	singe	traverse

1. The _____ of your idea makes it hard for me to comprehend what you mean; could you give me a concrete example?

2. The (argument) _____ between Jane and her friend developed over a difference of opinion about the safety of nuclear power.

3. "Whew! That sun is hot enough to _____ the hair on your head," Pat exclaimed as he dropped in front of the air conditioner.

4. Your terms are too _____; be more specific in the words you use.

5. Because I excused you for being late with your work today, do not _____ I will do so again.

6. Jeffrey _____ the hair on his arm while toasting marshmallows.

7. In the nineteenth century, Father DeSmet _____ the Atlantic Ocean to Europe and back more than a dozen times.

8. The horse that wins the Kentucky Derby was draped with beautiful _____ of flowers.

lesson 102

crisis ▪ splurge

crisis   (n)   (´krī-səs)

ORIGIN: Greek *krisis* (decision)

MEANING: A turning point, a decisive moment, or a crucial time in one's life, or in the state of affairs of people or nations

CONTEXT: "We are now facing a development *crisis* in the western United States; there will soon not be enough fresh water to go around."

SYNONYM: emergency

splurge   (v)   (splərj)

ORIGIN: Modern English

MEANING: To indulge oneself in some luxury, to spend money lavishly and in a showy manner

CONTEXT: "He *splurged* on expensive clothes both to satisfy his own desire and to impress his coworkers."

SYNONYMS: indulge oneself, show off

OTHER FORM: splurge (n.)

A. Focus on Meaning

Match each word with its synonym by writing the proper letter in the blank.

1.   crisis _____

2.   splurge _____

3.   abstract _____

4.   singe _____

5.   advocate _____

6.   aloof _____

a) conceptual   b) emergency   c) uninvolved   d) indulge oneself   e) favor   f) sear

B. Words in Context

Supply the proper form of the most appropriate vocabulary word.

crisis	novel	presume	splurge	tousle

1.   Although Pam later admitted that the eight thousand dollars she had _____ on a new car was a senseless indulgence, at the time she bought it no one could reason with her.

2.   I suggest that you try to devise a more _____ way to open your speech; telling that old joke is a dull beginning.

3.   President Kennedy's handling of the Cuban missile _____ will be remembered as an example of successful diplomacy.

4.   "Following your best friend's bad example and _____ on a motorcycle makes no sense, Mario," argued his mother.

5.   Benny Leonard, one of the all-time great lightweight boxing champions, used to enter the ring with his hair carefully slicked into place; miraculously, when he emerged, not one lock had become _____.

6.   He has passed the _____, and the doctors assure us that now he will get well.

7.   Leslie just naturally _____ that Brian had remembered to gas up the car before starting for Chicago.

lesson 103

-tract- ▪ poly-

-tract-	(root)		**poly-**	(prefix)
ORIGIN:	Latin *tractum* (to draw)		ORIGIN:	Greek *polys* (many)
MEANING:	To draw, drag, or pull		MEANING:	More than one, many
CONTEXT:	"*trac*tor"		CONTEXT:	"*Poly*gamy"

A. Focus on Meaning

In each of the italicized words below, underline the word parts that you have learned. Then, using your knowledge of the meanings of the word parts, circle the letter of the best meaning for the italicized word. (For some words there may be only one word part.)

1. a *tractable* person: a) stubborn   b) easily led   c) attractive   d) trusting

2. large *polygon*:   a) geometric figure having many sides   b) type of blood protein
c) business executive facing financial ruin   d) prehistoric animal

3. *retract* a statement: a) repeat   b) rewrite   c) take back   d) review

4. be more *circumspect*:   a) cautious by looking at a problem from all directions   b) prudent
c) selective   d) supportive

5. a complex *polynomial*:   a) apparatus   b) sentence
c) theory   d) algebraic expression with many terms

6. *distract* his attention: a) focus   b) draw away   c) encourage   d) discourage

7. *postgraduate* work: a) very gradual   b) before finishing college
c) after finishing college   d) after entering college

B. REVIEW

Match the correct definition to the vocabulary word. Write the letter of the definition on the line.

_____ 1. strife   a. rumple

_____ 2. invincible   b. intangible

_____ 3. presume   c. different

_____ 4. consecutive   d. conflict

_____ 5. abstract   e. continuous

_____ 6. tousle   f. scorch

_____ 7. singe   g. unconquerable

_____ 8. novel   h. assume

116   Lesson 103 • -TRACT-/POLY-

lesson 104

jubilant ▪ slack

jubilant (adj) (ˈjü-bə-lənt)

ORIGIN: Latin *jubilare* (to shout for joy)

MEANING: Showing great joy

CONTEXT: "Rosa was *jubilant* when we told her she could spend the summer at Grandfather's ranch."

SYNONYMS: joyful, exultant, elated

ANTONYMS: dejected, sorrowful

OTHER FORMS: jubilantly (adv.), jubilation (n.), jubilee (n.)

slack (adj) (slak)

ORIGIN: Old English *sleac* (slack)

MEANING 1: Not tight or firm; relaxed or weak

CONTEXT 1: "Because of *slack* discipline, the children believe they can do as they please."

MEANING 2: Lacking activity, dull

CONTEXT 2: "The inn manager says this spring has been a *slack* season for tourists because of the cold, wet weather."

SYNONYMS: weak, quiet, slow, sluggish

ANTONYMS: firm steady, diligent, active, busy

OTHER FORMS: slackly (adv.), slackness (n.)

A. Focus on Meaning

Match each word with its synonym by writing the proper letter in the blank.

1. jubilant _____

2. crisis _____

3. splurge _____

4. slack _____

5. jubilation _____

6. slackness _____

a) quiet   b) indulge oneself   c) sluggishness   d) elation   e) emergency   f) joyful

B. Words in Context

Supply the proper form of the most appropriate vocabulary word.

| abstract | jubilant | singe | slack | tousle |

1. A number of employees were laid off from work during a(n) _____ time at the factory.

2. When the Pirates won the World Series, wild _____ filled Pittsburgh, and the streets were buried in confetti.

3. The _____ training rules that the coach adopted will not strengthen the basketball team.

4. When I lit the fire in the fireplace, I _____ my tie.

5. Sandy, _____ over winning the essay contest, rushed around telling all her friends the good news.

6. Professor Jameson's _____ theories were difficult for me to understand until she explained them by giving concrete examples.

7. The team's dirty uniforms were _____ in such a heap it took the assistant couch an hour to get them untangled and ready to wash.

lesson 105

focus ▪ crevice

focus   (v)   (´fō-kəs)

ORIGIN: Latin *focus* (hearth)

MEANING: To cause to be concentrated on or adjusted to a particular place person, or thing

CONTEXT: "By holding the community meeting in the old building last week, we *focused* public attention on the need for a new library."

SYNONYMS: concentrate, converge, centralize

OTHER FORM: focus (n.)

crevice   (n)   (´krev-əs)

ORIGIN: Latin *crepare* (to crack)

MEANING: A narrow opening that is formed by a crack

CONTEXT: "The *crevice* in the rock was too narrow for James to squeeze through."

SYNONYMS: fissure, cranny, rift

A. Focus on Meaning

Circle the letter of the best meaning for each vocabulary word.

1. focus: a) frame   b) photograph   c) concentrate   d) fan
2. crevice: a) wild animal   b) crack   c) cave   d) vase
3. jubilant: a) depressed   b) intelligent   c) courageous   d) joyful
4. slack: a) slushy   b) dull   c) active   d) fearful
5. crevice: a) cover   b) step   c) cranny   d) boulder
6. focus: a) find   b) converge   c) scatter   d) climb

B. Words in Context

Supply the proper form of the most appropriate vocabulary word.

chasm   crevice   crisis   focus

1. The _____ in the cliff was large enough for us to walk into.
2. Interest is _____ on plans for the barbecue, the country-music festival, and the hoedown.
3. Keith was so sleepy that he could barely _____ his eyes on the TV.
4. Our country, according to many experts, is facing an energy _____, and drastic measures will have to be taken to prevent serious social consequences.
5. The _____ in the earth was widening, endangering a number of expensive homes near it.

C. Antonyms

Circle the letter of the word whose meaning is most nearly opposite the vocabulary word.

1. invincible   a) all-powerful   b) powerless   c) indomitable   d) radical
2. trivial   a) small   b) unimportant   c) significant   d) thick
3. consolidate   a) combine   b) merge   c) motivate   d) separate
4. novel   a) usual   b) unique   c) different   d) publication
5. abstract   a) intangible   b) concrete   c) conceptual   d) abundant
6. sparse   a) scanty   b) thin   c) thick   d) steady

lesson 106

verge ▪ rite

verge	(n)	(vərj)
ORIGIN:	Latin *vergere* (to bend)	
MEANING:	The limit or point beyond which something begins to happen	
CONTEXT:	"She was on the *verge* of a nervous breakdown when she decided to see a psychiatrist."	
SYNONYMS:	edge, brink, border, margin, point	

rite	(n)	(rīt)
ORIGIN:	Latin *ritus* (rite)	
MEANING:	A ceremonial or formal act or procedure	
CONTEXT:	"Each tribe had certain *rites* to perform when a member was buried."	
SYNONYMS:	ceremony, observance, form, service, sacrament	
OTHER FORM:	ritual (n.)	

A. Focus on Meaning

Circle the letter of the word in each group that does not belong.

1. a) verge   b) edge   c) view   d) border

2. a) rite   b) ceremony   c) observance   d) right

3. a) focus   b) form   c) concentrate   d) converge

4. a) crevice   b) crack   c) fissure   d) credit

5. a) rite   b) ceremony   c) privilege   d) sacrament

B. Words in Context

Supply the proper form of the most appropriate vocabulary word.

abstract	jubilant	novel	rite	slack	verge

1. The club has a strange _____ that members perform whenever a person is initiated into the secret society.

2. Work is so _____ at Dad's office right now that he is sure he can take a few days off and go with us to San Francisco.

3. The _____ of the coffee break has become as important to Americans as the custom of afternoon tea is to the British.

4. Dan was on the _____ of telling his mother the whole story when a knock at the door interrupted them.

5. Mary is _____ over the opportunity to visit her sister at the university.

6. We are on the _____ of making our cities unlivable because of pollution from automobile exhaust and industrial waste.

7. In the world of electronics it seems that there is an announcement of a _____ idea every day.

8. The essay on economic theory was too _____ for me.

lesson 107

convey ▪ fanatic

convey (v) (kən-ˊvā)

ORIGIN: Late Latin *conviare* (to accompany on the way)

MEANING: To carry, bring, or take from one place to another by means of transportation or communication

CONTEXT: "Large pipes *convey* water to the city from reservoirs."

SYNONYMS: carry, transport, transmit, bear, communicate

OTHER FORMS: conveyance (n.), equipment, conveyer (n.) person, conveyor (n.)

fanatic (n) (fə-ˊnat-ik)

ORIGIN: Latin *fanaticus* (inspired by a diety, frenzied)

MEANING: A person extremely enthusiastic and intensely zealous; one almost frenzied and uncritical in his or her devotion

CONTEXT: "During World War II members of the resistance movement in occupied Europe were *fanatics* in the cause of anti-Nazism; they believed that anyone who did not support them was a traitor."

SYNONYMS: zealot, radical, extremist, partisan

OTHER FORMS: fanatical (adj.), fanatically (adv.)

A. Focus on Meaning

Circle the letter of the word in each group that does not belong.

1. a) convey b) carry c) connect d) transport

2. a) fanatic b) zealot c) radical d) mediator

3. a) verge b) wall c) brink d) point

4. a) convey b) bear c) carry d) change

5. a) rite b) privilege c) ritual d) ceremony

6. a) fanatic b) moderate c) partisan d) zealot

B. Words in Context

Supply the proper form of the most appropriate vocabulary word.

convey	fanatic	focus	singe

1. "Will you _____ my best wishes to your sister when you see her?" asked Susan.

2. "I think you should continue to work for a change in the tax laws that penalize married couples who work," said the accountant, "but I hope you won't become _____ about it and lose all sense of perspective."

3. The only _____ we could find for the hay ride was an old wagon pulled by a tractor.

4. The newspaper editor tried to _____ public attention on the needs of handicapped citizens.

5. My St. Louis cousin, Carol, is a _____ about hockey; she has never missed a Blues home game.

6. Suddenly the flames shot out of the grill and _____ the left arm on my new sweater.

de- ■ -ful

de-	(prefix)	-ful	(suffix)
ORIGIN:	Latin *de* (from, down, away)	ORIGIN:	Old English *ful*
MEANING 1:	Down	MEANING:	Full of, characterized by
CONTEXT 1:	"*de*press"	CONTEXT:	"hope*ful*"
MEANING 2:	Away		
CONTEXT 2:	"*de*port"		
MEANING 3:	Reversing or undoing		
CONTEXT 3:	"*de*populate"		

A. Focus on Meaning

In each of the italicized words below, underline the word parts that you have learned. Then, using your knowledge of the meanings of the word parts, circle the letter of the best meaning for the italicized word. (For some words there may be only one word part.)

1. *degraded* by having to wash dishes: a) put down in dignity b) built up in dignity
   c) become bored d) became angry

2. a *cheerful* girl: a) lacking in cheer b) beautiful c) full of good spirits d) homesick

3. his leg in *traction*: a) at rest b) on a tractor c) held in splints or in a cast
   d) being drawn or pulled to help the bone grow straight

4. a *mournful* occasion: a) lacking grief b) full of grief c) rare d) past

5. *deactivate* the bomb: a) drop b) build
   c) take the possibility of action away from d) make active

6. to issue a *decree*: a) a newspaper b) money
   c) a rule handed down by an authority d) a rule based on kindness

B. REVIEW

Match the correct definition to the vocabulary word. Write the letter of the definition on the line.

_____ 1. consolidate   a. cranny

_____ 2. jubilant   b. combine

_____ 3. verge   c. bridge

_____ 4. slack   d. joyful

_____ 5. rite   e. concentrate

_____ 6. focus   f. border

_____ 7. traverse   g. ceremony

_____ 8. crevice   h. weak

lesson 109
debris ▪ forge

debris	(n)	(də-´brē)	
ORIGIN:	Old French *desbrisier* (to break apart)		
MEANING:	The remains of something destroyed or broken down		
CONTEXT:	"*Debris* from the old house was scattered about by the wind storm."		
SYNONYMS:	rubble, rubbish, wreckage, trash		

forge	(v)	(fō[ə]rj)
ORIGIN:	Latin *faber* (worker)	
MEANING 1:	To form, to make in any way, or to imitate (as a signature or handwriting)	
CONTEXT 1:	"He *forged* his father's name on the check."	
MEANING 2:	To move forward steadily and gradually; to progress	
CONTEXT 2:	"He *forged* ahead in his work and finished on time."	
SYNONYMS:	fabricate, make, invent, shape, fashion, imitate, counterfeit; progress	
OTHER FORMS:	forgery (n.), forger (n.)	

A. Focus on Meaning

Circle the letter of the best meaning for each vocabulary word.

1. debris: a) debts   b) rubbish   c) dishes   d) deer

2. forge: a) hammer   b) force   c) find   d) shape

3. convey: a) follow   b) communicate   c) complete   d) begin

4. debris: a) valuables   b) boxes   c) dents   d) trash

5. forge: a) imitate   b) burn   c) fill   d) empty

6. fanatic: a) clown   b) mourner   c) radical   d) helper

B. Words in Context

Supply the proper form of the most appropriate vocabulary word.

crevice	debris	forge	splurge	rite	verge

1. _____ from the packing crates covered the terrace as Shelly eagerly unwrapped the wedding presents.

2. The playing of taps is a part of the _____ of a military funeral.

3. "We are on the _____ of destroying ourselves with our own weapons," asserted the senator, who delivered a warning about the dangers of nuclear and biological warfare.

4. It is not right to _____ your mother's name on the excuse slip.

5. After the rock festival in the park, workers collected three truckloads of _____.

6. The rescue party _____ ahead through the dense underbrush, reaching the crash victims just before dark.

7. Instead of his usual two scoops of chocolate ice cream, Timmy _____ on a banana split.

8. Juan was able to stop the tennis ball as it was on the _____ of slipping down the _____ between the buildings.

lesson 110

tread ▪ ember

tread   (v)   (tred)

ORIGIN: Old English *tredan* (to tread)

MEANING: To step or walk on, about, in, or along; often to trample or crush underfoot

CONTEXT: "As you go through the garden, do not *tread* on the plants."

SYNONYMS: trample, walk, follow

ember   (n)   (´em-bər)

ORIGIN: Old English *aemerge* (ashes)

MEANING: The glowing fragment or small live coal from a fire, especially one smoldering in the ashes

CONTEXT: "We turned the glowing *embers* into a blaze by adding dry twigs and limbs to the coals."

A. Focus on Meaning

Circle the letter of the best meaning for each vocabulary word.

1. tread: a) climb   b) review   c) trample   d) prepare

2. ember: a) stone   b) light   c) small live coal   d) large flame

3. debris: a) teeth   b) rain   c) wind   d) trash

4. tread: a) jump   b) swim   c) hurtle   d) walk

5. forge: a) progress   b) protect   c) rescue   d) lose

B. Words in Context

Supply the proper form of the most appropriate vocabulary word.

convey   crisis   ember   fanatic   jubilant   tread

1. Do not _____ on the freshly waxed floor until it has been polished.

2. Aunt Marjorie was a(n) _____ about drinking milk; she insisted that my cousin consume a quart daily.

3. If you will put some kindling on the _____ in the fireplace, we can soon have a good fire going.

4. It is amazing how expert trackers can quietly _____ in the forest without disturbing so much as a single twig.

5. In some parts of Latin America, farmers still must use ox carts and burros to _____ their products to market.

6. All I could see in the darkness were the glowing _____ of our campfire.

7. Many scientists now believe that we are facing a _____ on Earth with global warming.

8. Tara was _____ to learn that she would have a part in the school play.

lesson 111

striking ▪ contempt

striking	(adj)	(´strīk-ing)	**contempt**	(n)	(kən-´tem[p]t)

ORIGIN:	Old English *strican* (to stroke)		ORIGIN:	Latin *con* (can) + *temnere* (to scorn)
MEANING:	Impressive, noticeably attractive		MEANING:	The feeling that one has toward anything considered mean, worthless, or vile; the act of despising
CONTEXT:	"How could you not notice a woman of such *striking* beauty?"		CONTEXT:	"I feel great *contempt* for cheating of all kinds."
SYNONYMS:	noticeable, remarkable, prominent, outstanding, conspicuous		SYNONYMS:	disdain, scorn, disapproval, detestation
ANTONYMS:	plain, unimpressive, unattractive		ANTONYMS:	approbation, respect, admiration, esteem
			OTHER FORMS:	contemptuous (adj.), contemptible (adj.)

A. Focus on Meaning

Circle the letter of the word or phrase in each group that does not belong.

1. a) striking   b) noticeable   c) impressive   d) dull

2. a) contempt   b) scorn   c) respect   d) disdain

3. a) tread   b) run   c) walk   d) trample

4. a) contempt   b) approval   c) scorn   d). disdain

5. a) embers   b) small burning coals   c) glowing remains of fire   d) roaring fire

B. Words in Context

Supply the proper form of the most appropriate vocabulary word.

contempt   debris   forge   striking

1. Mrs. Edmondson was not _____, but her warm personality set her apart from other women.

2. Ursula is _____ of anyone who does not participate in athletics.

3. Our highways are littered with _____ scattered by thoughtless motorists.

4. One of our neighbors was arrested for _____ when he attempted to cash a check to which he had signed a phony signature.

5. The _____ colors of the maples and chestnuts made them stand out from the other trees that we saw as we drove through the Ozark Mountains this fall.

6. Farmer Brown's _____ for the hunter who drove across the field of young corn to reach the woods was apparent.

Shades of Meaning

- noticeable
- remarkable
- prominent
- outstanding
- conspicuous

Noticeable applies to something that must be paid attention to. *Remarkable* applies to something that is noticed because it is unusual or exceptional. *Prominent* refers to something that stands out from its background. *Outstanding* refers to a person or thing that is remarkable as compared to others of its kind. *Conspicuous* applies to something that is so obvious that it is immediately seen.

lesson 112

re- ▪ -able

re- (prefix)

ORIGIN: Latin *re* (back, again)

MEANING: Back, again

CONTEXT: "*re*turn"

-able (suffix)

ORIGIN: Latin *abilis* (capable of)

MEANING: Capable of, fit for, worthy of, liable to, capable of being acted on

CONTEXT: "perish*able*"

OTHER FORM: -ible (collectible)

A. Focus on Meaning

In each of the italicized words below, underline the word parts that you have learned. Then, using your knowledge of the meanings of the word parts, circle the letter of the best meaning for the italicized word. (For some words there may be only one word part.)

1. *report* the accident: a) cause b) carry back information of c) remove all evidence of d) prevent

2. a *memorable* speech: a) memorized b) short c) worthy of being remembered d) not good enough to be remembered

3. *retrace* one's steps: a) erase b) make plainer c) go back over d) continue

4. *multiplex* suggestions: a) varied b) very many c) few d) especially good

5. above a *tolerable* level: a) low b) capable of being endured c) likely to be punished d) amusing

6. as the water *recedes*: a) rises b) goes back c) evaporates d) cools

7. *visible* signs: a) imagined b) hidden c) capable of being seen d) audible

8. *reconstituted* lemon juice: a) sour b) brought back together c) natural d) weak

B. REVIEW

Match the correct definition to the vocabulary word. Write the letter of the definition on the line.

_____ 1. congestion   a. make

_____ 2. debris   b. trample

_____ 3. disperse   c. overcrowding

_____ 4. forge   d. scorn

_____ 5. presume   e. transport

_____ 6. contempt   f. scatter

_____ 7. tread   g. rubbish

_____ 8. convey   h. assume

serene ▪ resound

serene　(adj)　(sə-ˊrēn)

ORIGIN:　Latin *serenus* (calm, peaceful)

MEANING:　Calm, peaceful, unruffled

CONTEXT:　"When I get upset and flustered, I go to see my neighbor who is always *serene* and has a calming effect on me."

SYNONYMS:　placid, tranquil, unperturbed, calm, composed

ANTONYMS:　excitable, disturbed, agitated

OTHER FORMS:　serenely (adv.), sereneness (n.), serenity (n.)

resound　(v)　(ri-ˊzaünd)

ORIGIN:　Latin *re* (again) + *sonare* (to sound)

MEANING:　To make an echoing sound or sound loudly

CONTEXT:　"The gong *resounded* to warn the people of the approach of the Mongol horde."

SYNONYMS:　reverberate, echo, peal, rebound, ring

OTHER FORMS:　resonant (adj.), resonance (n.)

A. Focus on Meaning

Match each word with its synonym by writing the proper letter in the blank.

1.　serene 　____
2.　resound ____
3.　striking ____

4.　contempt ____
5.　resonant ____
6.　serenity ____

a) ringing　　b) disdain　　c) peacefulness　　d) tranquil　　e) echo　　f) noticeable

B. Words in Context

Supply the proper form of the most appropriate vocabulary word

contempt	forge	resound	serene	tread

1.　The _____ thunder of the cannon that was fired after each touchdown at the football game could be heard all over town.

2.　Frank Lloyd Wright is noted for designing buildings of _____ beauty and simplicity.

3.　Grandfather's _____ for laziness was well known to us; therefore, we were always careful to appear busy when we were with him.

4.　It saddened me to learn that the _____ of the peaceful countryside was to be destroyed by the construction of a shopping center.

5.　How does Miss Wilson remain so _____ in that room full of first graders?

6.　The shots _____ through the valley, signaling that the lost children had been found.

7.　It is always interesting to watch glass blowers _____ glass flowers and animals.

8.　Angie _____ so lightly up the stairs that we did not hear her until she knocked on the door.

lesson 114

corrupt ▪ remorse

corrupt	(adj)	(kə-ˈrəpt)
ORIGIN:	Latin *corrumpere* (to destroy)	
MEANING:	Guilty of dishonest practices, wicked, evil	
CONTEXT:	"I have been told that he is a *corrupt* judge who can be bribed if one has the money."	
SYNONYMS:	wicked, debased, rotten, evil	
ANTONYMS:	innocent, upright, honorable, just	
OTHER FORMS:	corruption (n.), corruptness (n.), corruptly (adv.), corruptible (adj.), corrupt (v.)	

remorse	(n)	(ri-ˈmȯ[ə]rs)
ORIGIN:	Latin *re* (again) + *mordere* (to bite, sting, attack)	
MEANING:	Feeling deep and painful regret for wrongdoing	
CONTEXT:	"Danny's *remorse* caused him to tell me that he had stolen the book from my library."	
SYNONYMS:	regret, repentance, contrition	
OTHER FORMS:	remorseful (adj.), remorsefully (adv.), remorseless (adj.)	

A. Focus on Meaning

Circle the letter of the best meaning for each vocabulary word.

1. corrupt: a) wicked   b) correct   c) honorable   d) comical

2. remorse: a) removal   b) code   c) anger   d) regret

3. serene: a) sorrowful   b) calm   c) beautiful   d) agitated

4. corrupt: a) innocent   b) courteous   c) evil   d) contagious

5. remorse: a) repentance   b) sadness   c) happiness   d) agitation

6. resound: a) call   b) escape   c) sound   d) ring

B. Words in Context

Supply the proper form of the most appropriate vocabulary word.

> contempt   corrupt   remorse   serene   striking

1. Mr. Jones, formerly an honest politician, succumbed to temptation and has become _____.

2. Rob, _____ for having left Mother with so much Saturday cleaning to do, volunteered to fix dinner and wash the dishes.

3. The _____ government was overthrown and replaced by honest leaders.

4. Father had utter _____ for anyone who mistreated an animal.

5. The teacher became angry when the student showed no _____ for having forged her mother's name to an excuse note.

6. Maureen's red hair is the most _____ thing about her.

7. Sitting on the porch of Aunt Alice's cabin by the lake watching a mid-June sunset is the most _____ memory I have of my childhood.

defile ▪ obscure

defile	(v)	(di-ˈfī[ə]l)	**obscure**	(adj)	(ȧb-ˈskyu[ə]r)

defile (v) (di-ˈfī[ə]l)

ORIGIN: Old French *defouler* (to trample on)

MEANING: To make foul, dirty, impure; to sully or dishonor

CONTEXT: "Do not *defile* your good reputation by cheating on a test."

SYNONYMS: desecrate, sully, taint, pollute, corrupt

OTHER FORMS: defilable (adj.), defilingly (adv.), defilement (n.)

obscure (adj) (ȧb-ˈskyu[ə]r)

ORIGIN: Latin *obscurus* (covered over)

MEANING: Not distinct; not easily seen or understood

CONTEXT: "He must have some *obscure* motive for visiting an uncle he has always disliked, but I could not tell from his conversation what it was."

SYNONYMS: vague, remote, unclear, dim, hidden

ANTONYMS: certain, clear, conspicuous, evident

OTHER FORMS: obscure (v.), obscureness (n.), obscurity (n.)

A. Focus on Meaning

Circle the letter of the word in each group that does not belong.

1. a) defile   b) dirty   c) sully   d) honor

2. a) obscure   b) vague   c) certain   d) remote

3. a) corrupt   b) evil   c) immoral   d) honorable

4. a) obscure   b) secure   c) dim   d) unclear

5. a) defile   b) pollute   c) corrupt   d) define

B. Words in Context

Supply the proper form of the most appropriate vocabulary word.

corrupt	defile	obscure	resound	serene

1. The _____ of the woman's reputation resulted from the gossip started by a jealous acquaintance.

2. No matter how many frustrating things happened to our family, Mother always seemed to remain _____ and undisturbed.

3. Little is known of the young artist who came from a(n) _____ village in the mountains of eastern Kentucky.

4. The _____ of your biology report could be cleared up by the use of more precise terms and accurate statements.

5. On Sunday morning the valley _____ with the clear musical peal of the bell from our church steeple.

6. The mining company _____ the mountain streams and _____ local politicians to keep it quiet.

7. Andy was deeply _____ for accidentally stepping on Carrie's foot and breaking her toe.

justification ▪ slight

justification (n) (ˌjəs-tə-fə-ˈkā-shən)

ORIGIN: Latin *justificare* (to make just)

MEANING: A fact, a circumstance, an explanation, or a reason that defends or shows something to be right or reasonable

CONTEXT: "Her insulting remarks to him were ample *justification* for his leaving the party."

SYNONYMS: defense, vindication, exoneration, rightness

OTHER FORMS: justify (v.), justifiable (adj.)

slight (v) (slīt)

ORIGIN: Middle English *sleght*

MEANING: To treat as if of little importance, to ignore

CONTEXT: "Because Judy has her mind on the spring dance, she slights her studies."

SYNONYMS: neglect, ignore, disregard, rebuff, snub

ANTONYMS: consider, ponder

OTHER FORMS: slight (n.), slighting (adj.), slightingly (adv.)

A. Focus on Meaning

Circle the letter of the word in each group that does not belong.

1. a) justification   b) defense   c) shame   d) vindication
2. a) slight   b) neglect   c) ignore   d) consider
3. a) defile   b) defend   c) sully   d) taint
4. a) justification   b) exoneration   c) injustice   d) defense
5. a) slight   b) neglect   c) snub   d) help
6. a) obscure   b) understandable   c) vague   d) remote

B. Words in Context

Supply the proper form of the most appropriate vocabulary word.

corrupt   justification   remorse   slight

1. Do not feel that Christopher's failure to invite you to the party is an unforgivable _____; he might not have known you were back in town.
2. To defile your reputation by hanging around with that (dishonest) _____ crowd is very foolish.
3. I cannot _____ asking my parents for extra money because I have a very generous allowance supplemented by what I earn at my part-time job.
4. Tina felt _____ for having hurt Sarah's feelings and later called to apologize.
5. I believe that there is no _____ for capital punishment because statistics show that the death penalty has not slowed the homicide rate.

C. Antonyms

Circle the letter of the word whose meaning is most nearly opposite the vocabulary word.

1. contempt   a) scorn   b) admiration   c) disdain   d) pity
2. corrupt   a) debased   b) evil   c) rejected   d) honorable
3. jubilant   a) elated   b) joyful   c) dejected   d) playful
4. serene   a) composed   b) calm   c) disturbed   d) quiet
5. obscure   a) clear   b) vague   c) hidden   d) firm
6. striking   a) noticeable   b) steady   c) active   d) plain

lesson 117

sprightly ▪ ponder

sprightly (adj) (´sprīt-lē)

ORIGIN: Latin *spiritus* (spirit)

MEANING: Gay, lighthearted, lively, full of spirit

CONTEXT: "Joy is a *sprightly* little girl; she always seems to be happy and on the move."

SYNONYMS: spirited, blithe, spry, animated

ANTONYMS: dull, sluggish, cheerless

OTHER FORM: sprightliness (n.)

ponder (v) (´pȧn-dər)

ORIGIN: Latin *ponderare* (to weigh)

MEANING: To consider something thoroughly and carefully

CONTEXT: Because he did not wish to say anything hurtful, Dad *pondered* his words before speaking to his sister."

SYNONYMS: reflect, meditate, deliberate

A. Focus on Meaning

Match each word with its synonym by writing the proper letter in the blank.

1. sprightly _____   2. ponder_____   3. justification _____

4. sprightliness _____   5. afflict _____   6. slight _____

a) neglect   b) spryness   c) harass   d) meditate   e) spirited   f) defense

B. Words in Context

Supply the proper form of the most appropriate vocabulary word.

| defile   obscure   ponder   remorse   sprightly |

1. Julia said she was _____ how she might explain the dented car fender to Mom.

2. The old gentleman patrolling the park is as _____ as the squirrels darting about hunting fallen acorns.

3. Our grandfather warned us that we should never _____ the name of the Lord.

4. I often have to _____ awhile over a poem or an essay before I understand its full meaning.

5. The clouds _____ the view of the mountains.

6. Because of her _____ manner and animated talk, the students were surprised when they were told that Dr. Debo, the author who visited our class, is over eighty years old.

7. I found the essay on relativity so _____ that I had to read it three times, _____ every sentence before it began to make some sense to me.

8. To the very end the prisoner showed no _____ for the pain he caused his victims.

lesson 118

trait ▪ assert

trait	(n)	(trāt)	**assert**	(v)	(ə-ˈsərt)

trait (n) (trāt)

ORIGIN: Latin *trachere* (to draw)

MEANING: A distinguishing quality or characteristic, especially of personality

CONTEXT: "Not the least of Mike's good *traits* is his absolute honesty."

SYNONYMS: characteristic, peculiarity, quality, attribute

assert (v) (ə-ˈsərt)

ORIGIN: Latin *asserere* (to annex, to claim)

MEANING: To state clearly, strongly, and positively

CONTEXT: "Mr. Sims is the kind of person who *asserts* his opinion on a subject and then sits back and expects everyone to agree with him."

SYNONYMS: declare, affirm, avow

ANTONYMS: disclaim, deny, disavow

OTHER FORMS: assertion (n.), assertive (adj.)

A. Focus on Meaning

Circle the letter of the best meaning for each vocabulary word.

1. trait: a) characteristic   b) personality   c) deed   d) charm

2. assert: a) examine   b) write   c) declare   d) decline

3. sprightly: a) sluggish   b) pretty   c) loud   d) spirited

4. ponder: a) carry   b) deliberate   c) hurry   d) pound

5. assert: a) disclaim   b) avow   c) disavow   d) deny

6. trait: a) peculiarity   b) trust   c) quantity   d) danger

B. Words in Context

Supply the proper form of the most appropriate vocabulary word.

assert	justification	slight	trait

1. _____ of innocence is not enough; proof is necessary.

2. Although the president did not want to _____ any person who came out to welcome him, he did not have time to shake hands with everyone.

3. Among Mr. Fine's good character _____ are honesty, patience, and fairness.

4. What _____ can you give for not having your theme ready on time?

5. If you really think Janis should be dropped from the team, you should _____ your opinion.

6. Having the courage to stand up for what you believe is a character _____ I greatly admire.

Shades of Meaning

- assert
- declare
- affirm
- avow

Assert refers to stating something as true with great confidence but with no objective proof. *Declare* refers to stating something openly or formally, often in the face of opposition. *Affirm* implies deep conviction in one's statement and the likelihood that no one else will disagree. *Avow* implies an open, emphatic statement, often in support of other people.

lesson 119

confront ▪ spiral

confront	(v)	(kən-ʹfrənt)

ORIGIN:	Latin *com* (with) + *front* (forehead, front)
MEANING:	To come face to face with, to cause to meet
CONTEXT:	"The mob, when *confronted* by the police, decided to leave the building without trouble."
SYNONYMS:	face, oppose, defy, challenge
ANTONYMS:	avoid, submit, yield
OTHER FORM:	confrontation (n.)

spiral	(adj)	(ʹspī-rəl)

ORIGIN:	Latin *spira* (coil)
MEANING:	Advancing to a higher level through a series of circular movements or forms
CONTEXT:	"A beautiful *spiral* staircase leads to the second floor."
SYNONYMS:	coiled, winding
OTHER FORMS:	spiral (v.), spiral (n.), spiraling (adj.)

A. Focus on Meaning

Circle the letter of the word or phrase in each group that does not belong.

1. a) confront   b) face   c) connect   d) oppose

2. a) spiral   b) square   c) winding   d) coiled

3. a) trait   b) characteristic   c) attribute   d) trade

4. a) confrontation   b) meeting   c) opposition   d) withdrawal

5. a) spiral   b) coil   c) spite   d) twist upward

6. a) assert   b) declare   c) deny   d) affirm

B. Words in Context

Supply the proper form of the most appropriate vocabulary word.

assert	confront	ponder	slight	spiral	sprightly	trait

1. When _____ with the possibility of failing English, Van began to think about all the times he had slighted his studies.

2. As he _____ the matter, Van realized that he should have studied harder.

3. _____ of blue-and-white crepe paper, the club colors, decorated the columns at the front of the building.

4. After sustaining severe damage from antiaircraft fire, the bomber flipped on its wing and began a(n) _____ death dive.

5. Mr. Dixon, when _____ by his opponent, Mr. Goodman, admitted that he had made statements that might have defiled Goodman's character.

6. Michael felt _____ when she was not asked to Kathleen's birthday party.

7. "Tim," the coach said, " you have got to be more _____ if you want to be on the debate team."

8. One of Maryann's most endearing _____ is her _____ even when she is tired.

lesson 120

excel ▪ manor

excel   (v)   (ik-ˊsel)

ORIGIN: Latin *ex* (out of) + *cellere* (to rise)

MEANING: To outdo others (as in good qualities or ability); to surpass

CONTEXT: "Although Lynn is not very good in English, she *excels* in algebra."

SYNONYMS: perform in a superior way, exceed, surpass, outdo, outstrip

OTHER FORMS: excellent (adj.), excellence (n.)

manor   (n)   (ˊman-ər)

ORIGIN: Latin *manere* (to remain)

MEANING: An estate consisting of the main house and the land belonging to it

CONTEXT: "In early England, *manors* and rights over land and tenants were often granted to lords by the king."

SYNONYMS: plantation, mansion, villa

A. Focus on Meaning

Circle the letter of the best meaning for each vocabulary word.

1. excel: a) spoil   b) exceed   c) shorten   d) speed

2. manor: a) fashion   b) way   c) plantation   d) matter

3. confront: a) face   b) withdraw   c) expect   d) fire

4. spiral: a) staircase   b) road   c) cover   d) coil

5. manor: a) ruler   b) servant   c) mansion   d) but

6. excel: a) elate   b) excite   c) outdo   d) enact

7. embers: a) birds   b) smoldering fire   c) raging fire   d) hot steel

B. Words in Context

Supply the proper form of the most appropriate vocabulary word.

> assert   confront   excel   manor   ponder   trait

1. Her _____ grades made her eligible for a scholarship.

2. In England there are many beautiful _____ that are open to the public.

3. Herb has good ideas but is too timid to _____ them in class.

4. I have a recipe for corn lightbread that was brought to me by a descendant of a cook who worked at one of the southern _____.

5. Frankie _____ in football but is not so good in basketball.

6. Melinda's _____ of cheerfulness makes her a welcome member of any group.

7. Mother values peace in the family; she will go out of her way to avoid _____ with others.

8. Alec _____ the last question on the history test a long time before he wrote his answer.

LESSONS 101–120

For each numbered word choose the word or phrase that is closest in meaning to the vocabulary word. Write the letter for the word on the line provided.

1. forge   (a) avow   (b) outdo   1. _____
           (c) make   (d) fire up

2. contempt   (a) esteem   (b) respect   2. _____
           (c) scorn   (d) attack

3. confront   (a) avoid   (b) submit   3. _____
           (c) hide   (d) oppose

4. abstract   (a) tangible   (b) concrete   4. _____
           (c) unknown   (d) intangible

5. slack   (a) firm   (b) weak   5. _____
           (c) busy   (d) easy

6. convey   (a) carry   (b) cover   6. _____
           (c) exchange   (d) shape

7. corrupt   (a) innocent   (b) wicked   7. _____
           (c) honorable   (d) hidden

8. obscure   (a) conspicuous   (b) clear   8. _____
           (c) vague   (d) dark

9. excel   (a) exceed   (b) defy   9. _____
           (c) upset   (d) confirm

10. assert   (a) disclaim   (b) declare   10. _____
           (c) deny   (d) invent

11. ponder   (a) yield   (b) defend   11. _____
           (c) imitate   (d) deliberate

12. slight   (a) consider   (b) ponder   12. _____
           (c) neglect   (d) forget

13. serene   (a) agitated   (b) tranquil   13. _____

              (c) disturbed   (d) happy

14. focus   (a) show off   (b) concentrate   14. _____

              (c) find   (d) magnify

15. rite   (a) ceremony   (b) echo   15. _____

              (c) follow   (d) radical

16. tread   (a) tire   (b) ember   16. _____

              (c) track   (d) trample

17. splurge   (a) scorch   (b) service   17. _____

              (c) indulge oneself   (d) challenge

18. jubilant   (a) dejected   (b) sorrowful   18. _____

              (c) placid   (d) joyful

19. remorse   (a) respect   (b) regret   19. _____

              (c) vindication   (d) rebuff

20. debris   (a) rubbish   (b) evil   20. _____

              (c) cranny   (d) spiral

TEST TIPS ANWERS

Lessons 1-20   **_Lessons 41-60_**   **_Lessons 81-100_**

1. c   2. d   3. b   4. a   1. a   2. c   3. d   4. c   1. d   2. c   3. b

Lessons 21-40   **_Lessons 61-80_**

1. a   2. d   3. c   4. c   1. a   2. c   3. d

Answer Key

1 A. 1. c 2. a 3. b 4. d 5. a 6. d
   B. 1. spite 2. picket 3. spite
      4. pickets 5. picket 6. spiteful

2 A. l. b 2. a 3. d 4. c 5. a
   B. 1. picket 2. agility 3. spitefully
      4. swagger 5. agile 6. swaggered
      7. agility

3 A. 1. e 2. d 3. a 4. c 5. f 6. b
   B. 1. mortification 2. agility
      3. defective 4. swagger 5. mortify
      6. defect 7. spiteful 8. defective

4 A. 1. b 2. a 3. c 4. b 5. b
   B. 1. grim 2. sovereign
      3. agile 4. grim 5. swagger
      6. mortified, defective 7. grim

5 A. l. a 2. b 3. d 4. d 5. c
   B. 1. afflicted 2. defect 3. valor
      4. affliction 5. mortification
      6. valor 7. agility 8. Valiant

6 A. 1. e 2. d 3. a 4. b 5. c 6. f
   B. 1. tumult 2. grim 3. gaunt
      4. sovereign 5. tumult 6. gaunt

7 A. 1. c 2. a 3. b 4. a 5. d 6. c
   B. 1. tassel 2. negotiate 3. gaunt
      4. tassels 5. grim, afflicts
      6. negotiate 7. sovereign

8 A. 1. b 2. b 3. a 4. c 5. c
   B. 1. suspension 2. negotiate
      3. gaunt 4. tassels 5. suspend
      6. merge 7. valiantly 8. merge

9 Exercise 1. b 2. c 3. a 4. b 5. d
             6. d 7. c 8. b 9. d

10 A. 1. b 2. c 3. b 4. b 5. b
   B. 1. cringed 2. negotiate
      3. suspension 4. version
      5. picketed 6. mortification
   C. 1. c 2. b 3. d 4. d 5. c 6. a

11 A. 1. a 2. b 3. d 4. b 5. a
   B. 1. cringed 2. melancholy 3. pollute
      4. valor 5. pollute 6. melancholy
      7. tumultuous 8. suspended

12 A. 1. a 2. f 3. b 4. c 5. d 6. e
   B. 1. somber 2. version 3. Indulgent
      4. somber 5. melancholy
      6. pollution 7. indulged
      8. swaggered 9. somber

13 A. l. a 2. b 3. c 4. b 5. c 6. d
   B. 1. indulgence 2. martyrdom
      3. pollution 4. imperative
      5. cringe, valor 6. imperative
      7. martyrdom 8. versions

14 A. 1. b 2. b 3. a 4. b 5. a
   B. 1. hurtled 2. somber 3. magnitude
      4. indulge 5. hurtled 6. magnitude
      7. melancholy 8. magnitude

15 A. l. b 2. d 3. b 4. a 5. a
   B. 1. humiliation 2. liberalism
      3. martyr 4. liberal 5. Humility

16 A. 1. d 2. c 3. d 4. c 5. d
   B. 1. repulsive 2. laymen 3. magnitude
      4. repulsed 5. hurtled
   C. 1. b 2. c 3. a 4. a 5. d 6. d

17 A. 1. -less a 2. un- b 3. -less a
      4. un- c 5. -less a 6. -less c
      7. un- d 8. un- d 9. -less d
      10. un- b
   B. 1. f 2. b 3. c 4. h
      5. g 6. e 7. a 8. d

18 A. 1. a 2. f 3. b 4. d 5. e 6. c
   B. 1. layman 2. hoard 3. repulsed
      4. hordes 5. liberal 6. humility
      7. hoarded 8. hordes

19 A. 1. d 2. c 3. a 4. c 5. d 6. d
   B. 1. lateral 2. laity 3. inherited
      4. repulsed 5. hereditary
      6. somber 7. lateral 8. imperative

20 A. 1. a 2. d 3. d 4. c 5. b 6. a
   B. 1. knack 2. haughty 3. horde
      4. knack 5. magnitude
      6. haughtily 7. hurtles

Review / Test   Lessons 1-20

1. c 2. b 3. a 4. d 5. d 6. c 7. b 8. c
9. b 10. a 11. c 12. c 13. d 14. b 15. d
16. c 17. a 18. b 19. d 20. a

21 A. 1. b 2. a 3. a 4. b 5. a 6. c
   B. 1. picturesque 2. haughty
      3. picturesque 4. smirk 5. inherited

22 A. 1. -port- a 2. -fer- c 3. -less c
      4. -port- d 5. -fer- b 6. un- c
      7. -port- c
   B. 1. h 2. a 3. c 4. f
      5. e 6. g 7. d 8. b

23 A. 1. e 2. d 3. a 4. b 5. c 6. f
   B. 1. smirk 2. sheaf 3. punctuality
      4. knack 5. haughty 6. punctual
      7. humble 8. inherited

24 A. 1. b 2. b 3. c 4. c 5. a 6. b
   B. 1. apprentice 2. foul 3. smirk
      4. foul 5. apprenticeship 6. punctual
      7. layman 8. hoard

25 A. 1. d 2. c 3. d 4. d 5. c 6. d
   B. 1. destiny 2. allotted 3. destined
      4. allotment 5. punctual 6. sheafs
   C. 1. b 2. a 3. c 4. d 5. b 6. c

26 A. 1. sub- b 2. super- d 3. -port- c
      4. sub- c 5. -port- d 6. super- c
      7. sub- d
   B. 1. c 2. d 3. f 4. h
      5. a 6. e 7. g 8. b

27 A. l. a 2. c 3. b 4. b 5. a 6. d
   B. 1. domination 2. Vagabonds
      3. foul 4. dominated 5. vagabonds
      6. knack 7. laterally 8. dominate

28 A. 1. e 2. f 3. a 4. b 5. c 6. d
   B. 1. dormant 2. persevered
      3. destiny 4. dormant 5. persevered
      6. allotted 7. vagabonds

29 A. l. a 2. b 3. c 4. d 5. c 6. a
   B. 1. distinctive 2. Editorials
      3. vagabonds 4. dominates
      5. edit 6. swaggering, distinctive
      7. heredity 8. picturesque

30 A. 1. c 2. b 3. c 4. c 5. a 6. a
   B. 1. foliage 2. cantankerous
      3. haughtiness 4. dormant
      5. foliage 6. cantankerous
      7. apprentice, persevere 8. dominant

31 A. 1. -ben- c 2. -sup- d 3. -ben- c
      4. pro- b 5. super- d 6. pro- c
   B. 1. b 2. c 3. a 4. e
      5. d 6. h 7. g 8. f

32 A. 1. c 2. b 3. b 4. a 5. b
   B. 1. stimulate 2. foliage 3. prophecy
      4. edited 5. stimulated 6. fouled
      7. prophesied, destinies 8. stimulated

33 A. 1. f 2. c 3. a 4. b 5. d 6. e
   B. 1. professes 2. bureaucrats
      3. cantankerous 4. professed
      5. distinctive 6. bureaucracy
      7. allot, edit 8. professes

34 A. 1. b 2. d 3. a 4. b 5. d 6. a
   B. 1. casualness 2. stimulate
      3. fiendish 4. Casual
      5. prophesied 6. fiend
   C. 1. d 2. a 3. b 4. c 5. c 6. d

35 A. l. b 2. c 3. d 4. a 5. a 6. d
   B. 1. averted 2. casual 3. professed
      4. avert 5. ruddy 6. foliage
      7. stimulate, ruddy
      8. averted, bureaucracy

36 A. 1. -sta- d 2. -ben-, -dict- a
      3. -ben- a 4. -stat- b 5. -dict- c
      6. pro- c 7. -stat- c 8. -sist- a
      9. un- d
   B. 1. e 2. h 3. a 4. b
      5. d 6. g 7. f 8. c

37 A. 1. c 2. d 3. c 4. c 5. d 6. d
   B. 1. bestowal 2. via 3. casual
      4. via 5. fiend 6. bestowed

38 A. 1. c 2. b 3. c 4. b 5. b
   B. 1. ally 2. vibrate 3. allied
      4. avert 5. vibrant 6. distinctive
      7. professed 8. bestowed

39 A. 1. b 2. b 3. c 4. c 5. b 6. c
   B. 1. domesticated 2. teem
      3. bestowed 4. teeming 5. casual
      6. domesticated 7. fiend

40 A. 1. intra- b 2. inter- d 3. -stat- c
      4. intro- c 5. -dict- d 6. inter- b
      7. pro- b 8. intra- b
   B. 1. d 2. a 3. f 4. g
      5. h 6. b 7. c 8. e

Review / Test   Lessons 21-40

1. b 2. d 3. c 4. c 5. a 6. b 7. c 8. d
9. b 10. c 11. d 12. b 13. a 14. b 15. c
16. d 17. c 18. b 19. a 20. c

41 A. 1. a 2. d 3. d 4. d 5. b
   B. 1. rendition 2. vibrations
      3. attired 4. ally 5. render
      6. attire 7. via, averted 8. teemed

42 A. 1. b 2. a 3. a 4. a 5. d
   B. 1. impenetrable 2. teemed
      3. domestic 4. awe 5. penetrate
      6. awesome 7. alliance

43 A. 1. c 2. b 3. c 4. b 5. a 6. d
   B. 1. tempestuous 2. attire
      3. ascribed 4. rendered
      5. ascribed 6. tempest
   C. 1. c 2. b 3. d 4. b 5. a 6. b

44 A. 1. -mit- c 2. -ject- b 3. inter- c
      4. sub-, -mit- a 5. sub-, -ject- c
      6. intra- a 7. -dict- d 8. -mit- c
      9. -miss- b
   B. 1. c 2. g 3. f 4. e
      5. h 6. b 7. a 8. d

45 A. 1. b 2. e 3. f 4. c 5. d 6. a
   B. 1. zeal 2. penetrates 3. awe
      4. zealous 5. covetous 6. covet

46 A. 1. c 2. b 3. c 4. a 5. a
   B. 1. copes 2. ascribed 3. reliance
      4. tempest 5. reliable 6. awe, attire
      7. Render 8. coped, penetrating

47 A. 1. c 2. c 3. a 4. c 5. d 6. b
   B. 1. anecdotes 2. antidote 3. covet
      4. via 5. lateral 6. zealous
      7. antidote 8. anecdotes

48 A. 1. b 2. d 3. c 4. c 5. b 6. d
   B. 1. exploitation 2. query
      3. Reliable 4. exploits 5. query
      6. zealously 7. ascribed, anecdotes
      8. rely, cope

49 A. 1. -cap- c 2. -duce- b 3. -cep- b
      4. -duc- b 5. -mit- c 6. -duct- d
      7. inter-, -ject- c 8. -cap- c
   B. 1. f 2. a 3. g 4. d
      5. h 6. e 7. b 8. c

50 A. 1. b 2. e 3. a 4. f 5. d 6. c
   B. 1. assailant 2. coveting
      3. exploited 4. query
      5. queried 6. quest
      7. indulged 8. assailed

51 A. 1. c 2. b 3. c 4. d 5. c
   B. 1. jaunty 2. chasm 3. exploit
      4. gaunt 5. jaunty 6. chasm

52 A. 1. b 2. a 3. c 4. a 5. d 6. a
   B. 1. arid 2. enlighten 3. jaunty
      4. chasm 5. enlightenment
      6. antidote 7. arid 8. coveting

53 A. 1. d 2. d 3. d 4. b 5. c
   B. 1. reservoir 2. query 3. foster
      4. jaunty 5. zealously 6. foster
      7. assailed, reservoir 8. reliability

54 A. 1. -graph- c 2. -scrib- c
      3. -graph- b 4. -cap- a 5. -scrib- c
      6. -graph- d 7. -mit- c 8. gram- c
   B. 1. c 2. e 3. h 4. g
      5. a 6. f 7. d 8. b

55 A. 1. b 2. c 3. a 4. a 5. b
   B. 1. arid 2. enlightened 3. clambering
      4. clamber 5. obstinately

56 A. 1. c 2. d 3. a 4. d 5. b 6. b
   B. 1. ardent 2. orator 3. obstinate
      4. reservoir 5. foster 6. oratorical
      7. anecdotes, exploits 8. queries
      9. ardent

57 A. 1. b 2. e 3. a 4. f 5. d 6. c
   B. 1. comply 2. obstinate 3. utensils
      4. compliance 5. Clambering
      6. obstinate 7. vibrated 8. assailed
   C. 1. d 2. a 3. d 4. b 5. c 6. c

58 A. 1. mis- c 2. contra- a
      3. contra- b 4. -duct- c
      5. -graph- c 6. counter- b
   C. 1. e 2. a 3. h 4. d
      5. f 6. b 7. g 8. c

59 A. 1. d 2. d 3. a 4. a 5. d
   B. 1. rave 2. oration 3. controversy
      4. ardently 5. controversy
      6. raving 7. quest 8. enlightened

60 A. 1. d 2. c 3. d 4. b 5. c 6. d
   B. 1. bounteous 2. prevailed
      3. comply 4. prevalent
      5. bounteousness 6. utensil
      7. foster 8. jauntily

Review / Test   Lessons 41-60

1. b 2. c 3. a 4. d 5. d 6. b 7. c 8. c
9. b 10. b 11. c 12. a 13. d 14. b 15. c
16. d 17. a 18. b 19. c 20. d

61 A. 1. c 2. b 3. a 4. a 5. d
   B. 1. advocates 2. rave 3. curtailment
      4. controversy 5. curtail 6. advocate
      7. clambered 8. reservoir

62 A. 1. a 2. d 3. c 4. a 5. c 6. d
   B. 1. Celestial 2. groping 3. prevail
      4. bounteous 5. comply 6. arid
      7. celestial 8. groped

63 A. 1. in- b 2. di- c 3. mis- a 4. im- a
      5. di- b 6. dis- d 7. in-, -ject- b
      8. dis- b 9. counter- a
   B. 1. g 2. f 3. a 4. h
      5. d 6. e 7. b 8. c

64 A. 1. f 2. c 3. a 4. b 5. e 6. d
   B. 1. maze 2. curtail 3. indifference
      4. maze 5. indifferent 6. advocate
      7. version 8. obstinately
      9. maze, chasms 10. indifferent

65 A. 1. d 2. a 3. d 4. b 5. b
   B. 1. adjacent 2. celestial 3. discredit
      4. adjacent 5. discredit

66 A. 1. b 2. a 3. d 4. d 5. a 6. c
   B. 1. diversion 2. comply 3. aloof
      4. diverted 5. maze
   C. 1. a 2. d 3. a 4. c 5. b 6. c

67 A. 1. multi- a 2. -pon- a 3. multi- d
      4. mis- b 5. -posit- a 6. multi- b
   B. 1. c 2. a 3. g 4. h
      5. e 6. d 7. b 8. f

68 A. 1. e 2. f 3. a 4. b 5. c 6. d
   B. 1. conspiracy 2. dispersed
      3. adjacent 4. conspired
      5. discredit 6. dispersed
      7. groping 8. curtailed

69 A. 1. b 2. a 3. b 4. c 5. b
   B. 1. conspiracy 2. vitality
      3. suppression 4. diverted
      5. vitality 6. suppress
      7. bounteous 8. advocate

70 A. 1. b 2. c 3. d 4. a 5. b 6. a
   B. 1. whetted 2. insomniac 3. vitality
      4. insomnia 5. whetted 6. suppress
      7. maze 8. aloof

71 A. 1. -ten- c   2. -ten- c   3. -ten- c
   4. -tain- c   5. -tent- a   6. multi- b
   7. -tin- a
   B. 1. h   2. d   3. g   4. b
   5. a   6. c   7. f   8. e

72 A. 1. b   2. d   3. b   4. b   5. d   6. c
   B. 1. vitality   2. chafed   3. suppressed
   4. gait   5. chafing   6. gait
   7. indifferent   8. divert

73 A. 1. b   2. b   3. d   4. a   5. c
   B. 1. harassed   2. insomnia   3. whetted
   4. chafe   5. gait   6. etiquette
   7. harassed, dispersed   8. insomnia

74 A. 1. d   2. c   3. c   4. a   5. d
   B. 1. gait   2. grappling   3. conspiring
   4. tassel   5. attire   6. integrity

75 A. l. a   2. f   3. b   4. c   5. e   6. d
   B. 1. etiquette   2. wrath   3. integrity
   4. harassed   5. instigated   6. wrathfully
   7. divert, instigator   8. whet

76 A. 1. -spect- d   2. in-, con- c
   3. -spec- c   4. inter-, -pose- c
   5. col- d   6. -spec- c   7. -tens- c
   B. 1. b   2. d   3. h   4. f
   5. g   6. e   7. c   8. a

77 A. l. a   2. c   3. b   4. c   5. b
   B. 1. bigot   2. wrath   3. integrity
   4. bigotry   5. contemplation
   C. 1. b   2. c   3. d   4. b   5. a   6. d

78 A. 1. d   2. c   3. f   4. b   5. a   6. e
   B. 1. essential   2. compelled
   3. wrathful   4. instigated
   5. compelled   6. essence   7. chafed

79 A. 1. d   2. a   3. a   4. a   5. a   6. d
   B. 1. comprehension   2. contemplate
   3. pretentious   4. bigotry
   5. pretenses   6. grappled
   7. etiquette   8. comprehend

80 A. 1. d   2. d   3. d   4. b   5. c
   B. 1. combustion   2. tedious   3. essence
   4. pretense   5. comprehend
   6. contemplating   7. comprehending
   8. tedious

Review / Test   Lessons 61-80

1. c   2. c   3. b   4. a   5. d   6. c   7. a   8. b
9. d   10. a   11. b   12. c   13. d   14. b   15. a
16. d   17. b   18. c   19. d   20. a

81 A. 1. semi- b   2. -spec- c   3. mono- b
   4. demi- c   5. -tens- c   6. mono- d
   7. hemi- c
   B. 1. d   2. f   3. g   4. e
   5. b   6. a   7. c   8. h

82 A. 1. b   2. c   3. a   4. e   5. d   6. f
   B. 1. trends   2. trend   3. pretense
   4. compelled   5. consecrated
   6. consecration

83 A. 1. b   2. a   3. c   4. b   5. a   6. c
   B. 1. prudent   2. erred   3. tedious
   4. prudence   5. combustible
   C. 1. c   2. b   3. a   4. d   5. c   6. a

84 A. 1. a   2. c   3. c   4. d   5. b   6. a
   B. 1. unquenchable   2. trend
   3. consecration   4. congestion
   5. congested   6. compel, comprehend
   7. err   8. essential

85 A. 1. -corp- d   2. -corpor- d
   3. in-, com- b   4. -gen- b
   5. pro-, -gen- b   6. -corp- b
   7. -gen- c
   B. 1. e   2. a   3. c   4. h
   5. f   6. g   7. b   8. d

86 A. l. a   2. c   3. c   4. d   5. b
   B. 1. agitated   2. erred   3. widespread
   4. agitating   5. Widespread
   6. tedious   7. widespread trend
   8. combustible

87 A. 1. b   2. f   3. a   4. c   5. e   6. d
   B. 1. scoffed   2. graft   3. congestion
   4. quenches   5. graft   6. scoffed
   7. prudent   8. consecrated

88 A. 1. c   2. a   3. c   4. b   5. d   6. c
   B. 1. consecutive   2. alternate
   3. consecutive   4. widespread
   5. agitate   6. alternate
   7. congestion   8. prudently

89 A. 1. -fic- b   2. -gress- a   3. -fic- a
   4. mono- b   5. -grad- b   6. -fac- c
   B. 1. d   2. h   3. f   4. b
   5. g   6. c   7. a   8. e

90 A. 1. c   2. b   3. b   4. a   5. a
   B. 1. compromise   2. intrude
   3. compromise   4. scoff
   5. intrusion   6. quenched   7. graft

91 A. 1. a   2. d   3. b   4. b   5. b
   B. 1. Graciousness   2. abide
   3. consecutive   4. abide

92 A. l. a   2. c   3. a   4. b   5. a
   B. 1. turf   2. gentility   3. genteel
   4. turf   5. intruded   6. alternates
   7. compromised   8. abide

93 A. 1. b   2. d   3. c   4. c   5. d
   B. 1. sparse   2. invincibility   3. bigots
   4. genteel   5. sparseness
   C. 1. d   2. h   3. c   4. a   5. d   6. c

94 A. 1. trans- b   2. circum- c   3. trans- c
   4. circum- c   5. -gen- c
   6. trans-, -pose- d   7. circum- d
   B. 1. b   2. c   3. d   4. f
   5. g   6. h   7. e   8. a

95 A. 1. d   2. f   3. b   4. e   5. a   6. c
   B. 1. genteel   2. data   3. data
   4. traversed   5. foster   6. traversed
   7. intrusion   8. gracious

96 A. 1. a   2. c   3. b   4. b   5. c
   B. 1. garland   2. agitating   3. sparse
   4. invincible   5. garlands   6. trivial
   7. genteel   8. trivia

97 A. 1. c   2. a   3. b   4. a   5. d   6. d
   B. 1. consolidation   2. traverse
   3. radical   4. consolidate
   5. radical, invincible
   6. data, sparse   7. consolidated

98 A. 1. pre- b   2. post-, -pon- c   3. pre- b
   4. trans-, -gress- c   5. post- b
   6. pre- c   7. trans- b
   C. 1. e   2. h   3. a   4. c
   5. f   6. b   7. d   8. g

99 A. 1. c   2. c   3. b   4. b   5. d
   B. 1. presumed   2. strife   3. garland
   4. strife   5. presumed
   6. consolidated   7. trivial
   8. presumed

100 A. 1. c   2. d   3. f   4. e   5. b   6. a
   B. 1. radical   2. novelty   3. tousled
   4. consolidated   5. novel   6. tousle

Review / Test   Lessons 81-100

1. d   2. a   3. c   4. c   5. b   6. d   7. c   8. a
9. b   10. d   11. c   12. a   13. c   14. b   15. d
16. d   17. a   18. b   19. c   20. c

101 A. 1. c   2. c   3. c   4. d   5. b
   B. 1. abstractness   2. controversy
   3. singe   4. abstract   5. presume
   6. singed   7. traversed   8. garland

102 A. 1. b   2. d   3. a   4. f   5. e   6. c
   B. 1. splurged   2. novel   3. crisis
   4. splurging   5. tousled   6. crisis
   7. presumed

103 A. 1. -tract- b   2. poly- a   3. -tract- c
   4. circum-, -spec- a   5. poly- d
   6. dis-, -tract- b   7. post-, -grad- c
   B. 1. d   2. g   3. h   4. e
   5. b   6. a   7. f   8. e

104 A. 1. f   2. e   3. b   4. a   5. d   6. c
   B. 1. slack   2. jubilation   3. slack
   4. singed   5. jubilant   6. abstract
   7. tousled

138   Answer Key

105 A. 1. c 2. b 3. d 4. b 5. c 6. b
B. 1. crevice 2. focused 3. focus
   4. crisis 5. chasm
C. 1. b 2. c 3. d 4. a 5. b 6. c

106 A. 1. c 2. d 3. b 4. d 5. c
B. 1. rite 2. slack 3. rite 4. verge
   5. jubilant 6. verge 7. novel
   8. abstract

107 A. 1. c 2. d 3. b 4. d 5. b 6. b
B. 1. convey 2. fanatical 3. conveyance
   4. focus 5. fanatic 6. singed

108 A. 1. de-, -grad- a 2. -ful c 3. -tract- d
   4. -ful b 5. de- c 6. de- c
B. 1. b 2. d 3. f 4. h
   5. g 6. e 7. c 8. a

109 A. 1. b 2. d 3. b 4. d 5. a 6. c
B. 1. Debris 2. rite 3. verge
   4. forge 5. debris 6. forged
   7. splurged 8. verge, crevice

110 A. 1. c 2. c 3. d 4. d 5. a
B. 1. tread 2. fanatic 3. embers
   4. tread 5. convey 6. embers
   7. crisis 8. jubilant

111 A. 1. d 2. c 3. b 4. b 5. d
B. 1. striking 2. contemptuous
   3. debris 4. forgery 5. striking
   6. contempt

112 A. 1. re-, -port- b 2. -able c 3. re- c
   4. multi- b 5. -able b 6. re- b
   7. -ible c 8. re-, con-, sti- b
B. 1. c 2. g 3. f 4. a
   5. h 6. d 7. b 8. e

113 A. 1. d 2. e 3. f 4. b 5. a 6. c
B. 1. resounding 2. serene
   3. contempt 4. serenity
   5. serene 6. resounded
   7. forge 8. treaded

114 A. 1. a 2. d 3. b 4. c 5. a 6. d
B. 1. corrupt 2. remorseful 3. corrupt
   4. contempt 5. remorse
   6. striking 7. serene

115 A. 1. d 2. c 3. d 4. b 5. d
B. 1. defilement 2. serene 3. obscure
   4. obscureness 5. resounded
   6. defiled, corrupt 7. remorseful

116 A. 1. c 2. d 3. b 4. c 5. d 6. b
B. 1. slight 2. corrupt 3. justify
   4. remorse 5. justification
C. 1. b 2. d 3. c 4. c 5. a 6. d

117 A. 1. e 2. d 3. f 4. b 5. c 6. a
B. 1. pondering 2. sprightly 3. defile
   4. ponder 5. obscured 6. sprightly
   7. obscure, pondering 8. remorse

118 A. 1. a 2. c 3. d 4. b 5. b 6. a
B. 1. Assertion 2. slight 3. traits
   4. justification 5. assert 6. trait

119 A. 1. c 2. b 3. d 4. d 5. c 6. c
B. 1. confronted 2. pondered
   3. Spirals 4. spiraling 5. confronted
   6. slighted 7. assertive
   8. traits, sprightliness

120 A. 1. b 2. c 3. a 4. d 5. c 6. c 7. b
B. 1. excellent 2. manors 3. assert
   4. manors 5. excels 6. trait
   7. confrontations 8. pondered

Review / Test   Lessons 101-120

1. c 2. c 3. d 4. d 5. b 6. a 7. b 8. c
9. a 10. b 11. d 12. c 13. b 14. b 15. a
16. d 17. c 18. d 19. b 20. a

Pronunciation Key

ə....*a*bout   ā....h*a*te   ē....*e*vening   ī....p*i*pe   ȯ....p*a*w

[ə]....met*a*l   e....m*e*t   i....d*i*p   ō....*o*ver   ü....p*u*ll

a....h*a*t   ȧ....c*o*d

′....mark preceding a syllable with primary stress

ı....mark preceding a syllable with secondary stress

[]....indicates that symbol contained within brackets is given very light stress

⁻....marks syllable division

Index